the test ban treaty:

military, technological, and political implications

James Hubert McBride

the
test ban treaty:

military, technological, and political implications

Henry Regnery Company · Chicago

*For
Jamie,
George,
Bill,
and John*

foreword

The purpose of this study is to analyze the impact of the Nuclear Test Ban Treaty, signed in Moscow on August 5, 1963, on the future security of the United States. The study discusses three aspects of the treaty: military, technological, and political. The immediate background for the study is the two separate hearings held on the treaty by the Senate Foreign Relations Committee and the Preparedness Investigating Subcommittee of the Senate Armed Services Committee, and official statements made by members of both the executive and the legislative branches of the government.

The first chapter establishes the rationale for the study and discusses the two hearings and committee reports. It is interesting to note that the two committees came to opposite conclusions concerning the treaty. Chapter II sketches the historical background of the treaty. Chapter III then describes and compares the comparative levels of nuclear technology in the United States and the Soviet Union as of the summer of 1963. First the Soviet and American post-moratorium test series are described and compared; then the comparative positions of the United States and the Soviet Union are discussed in terms of high yield technology, intermediate range, submegaton range, nuclear weapons effects, antiballistic missiles, and penetration. The next two chapters are concerned with the problem of clandestine testing as it applies to this limited treaty and some strategic military problems that will be affected by the restrictions on nuclear testing.

Chapter VI provides an analysis of the treaty in terms of the military and technological advantages and disadvantages which it portends for the United States. Twenty-three risks or disadvantages are uncovered, while the advantages claimed for it by official witnesses before the two committees are examined and found to be unpersuasive. Chapter VII

145518

discusses the safeguards demanded by the Joint Chiefs of Staff and promised by the political leadership, and analyzes their impact upon the risks and disadvantages uncovered in the preceding chapter.

Chapter VIII treats the political aspects of the treaty. The political advantages publicly claimed for the treaty by key political figures in the executive branch are discussed and analyzed. Of the four political advantages claimed for the treaty, only one is found to be persuasive, and it is of very limited validity. Two of the claimed advantages, when analyzed, prove to be disadvantages.

In view of the military, technological, and political disadvantages of the treaty and the absence of offsetting advantages, it is concluded that the Nuclear Test Ban Treaty is prejudicial to the security of the United States.

JAMES H. McBRIDE
Ann Arbor, Michigan, 1967

acknowledgments

I am greatly indebted to a number of distinguished individuals who played important roles in the Senate hearings on the Test Ban Treaty for their advice, assistance, and encouragement in writing this dissertation. Included in this group are Mr. Richard V. Allen, Admiral Arleigh A. Burke, Mr. J. Fred Bushardt, Mr. Russell J. Fee, and General Nathan F. Twining. I would also like to express my appreciation to the Center for Strategic Studies, Georgetown University, who helped make this study possible. Special mention should be made of Dr. James D. Atkinson, Georgetown University, who read the entire manuscript carefully and offered many helpful suggestions for revision and improvement. While much is owed to many, all expressions of opinion and errors of commission and omission are mine alone.

James H. McBride

table of contents

chapter 1

INTRODUCTION

It is generally agreed that the Test Ban Treaty, signed in Moscow on August 5, 1963, is one of the most important treaties of the twentieth century. Certainly it is the most significant arms control treaty of the nuclear age thus far. The Honorable Arthur Dean, former U.S. Ambassador to the Eighteen Nation Disarmament Conference, said:

> I think this particular treaty is probably as important if not the most important [sic], treaty in relation to our national survival which probably has ever been negotiated by the Administration or submitted to the Senate for its advice and consent.[1]

And during the Senate debate on the treaty, Senator Stuart Symington, former Secretary of the Air Force, said: "It is my judgement that the action taken by the Senate on this treaty could well be its most important action during our time."[2]

But while there is general agreement that the treaty is a milestone in postwar diplomacy, there has been widespread and vigorous disagreement as to its desirability from the viewpoint of national security. Public interest ran so high during the Senate debate on the treaty that Senator Everett M. Dirksen, Senate Minority Leader, commented: "I doubt that at any other time—except three—in nearly thirty years of experience in the House and in the Senate, have I been so beset with the views and expressions of people every-

---

[1] U.S. Congress, Senate Committee on Foreign Relations, *Hearings on the Nuclear Test Ban Treaty,* 88th Cong., 1st Sess., 1963, pp. 813-14. Hereafter cited as *Foreign Relations Committee Hearings.*

[2] *Congressional Record* (daily edition), 88th Cong., 1st Sess., September 17, 1963, p. 16256.

where."[3] Despite the great public interest and heated controversy, however, there was little solid information available to the public upon which to base a thorough and objective study of the treaty's implications for national security until well after it was ratified and 102 nations had acceded to it.

One reason this information was not available is that it involved highly classified military, technological, and intelligence information not normally released to the public for reasons of security. Another reason was that any comprehensive analysis of the impact of the treaty on the future security of the nation would require a broad range of facts and judgments that could be provided only by the nation's top military, technical, and political experts. Independent scholars and analysts simply cannot assemble these key personnel and interrogate them, nor are these people free to present their private views to the public. Nevertheless, in a democracy such as ours the public should have available to it an independent, unclassified analysis of the impact of the Test Ban Treaty, based upon essentially the same body of information that was available to the executive branch of the government. It is the purpose of this study to make such an analysis.

But, it might be asked, since the President and his principal advisors apparently concluded that the treaty did not imperil the national security, why should an independent study be made? There are two reasons. First, if comprehensive studies were made by the Department of State, the Arms Control and Disarmament Agency, the Department of Defense, the Atomic Energy Commission, the Joint Chiefs of Staff, or the Committee of Principals, they are not available for public scrutiny; nor can it be said with certainty that such studies were made. The second reason is well ex-

---

[3] *Ibid.*, September 11, 1963, p. 15912.

pressed by Herman Kahn in his book *Thinking About the Unthinkable:*

> Most people do not appreciate just how ill-equipped our government is to perform long range planning. The most able officials are constantly involved in the meeting of day-to-day crises, Congressional investigations, budgetary problems, and administrative detail, with little time to devote to the long range problems. . . .[4]

In other words, it is quite possible that, because of the pressures of day-to-day business, the rapid march of events leading up to the treaty, and the enormous complexities involved in assembling and analyzing the pertinent facts and judgments, a really thorough and complete job was not accomplished prior to the signing of the treaty. Precisely what went on behind the closed doors of the various departments, agencies, and committees that were involved in the final decision to negotiate the treaty, and how it came to be written as it was, has not yet been revealed. It seems appropriate, therefore, that an independent analysis of the long-range impact of the Test Ban Treaty be undertaken, even though the treaty is an accomplished fact. There may be no choice but to live with it, but it is well to know just what we are living with, and how it will affect us.

In determining the implications of the Test Ban Treaty, it should be noted that there are three kinds, or orders, of factors involved: military, technological, and political. These three factors are so closely related that it is difficult, if not impossible, to separate them into clean, neat compartments. The military and technological factors are particularly difficult to separate, since today's technology is tomorrow's military hardware. For this reason the military and technological factors should be treated together, with no attempt at

---

[4] Herman Kahn, *Thinking About the Unthinkable* (New York: Avon Books, 1962), p. 35.

separation. Political factors, while closely related to and interacting with the other two, can more readily and profitably be isolated for analytical purposes. Accordingly, Chapters III through VII will be directed to military and technological factors, while Chapter VIII will treat the political.

In approaching a study of this nature, the first task is to pose a series of questions to which the developed study should provide reasonable answers. The broad questions that formed the guidelines of the search for authoritative and relevant information were as follows:

1. What is the relative state of the art in the United States and the Soviet Union with respect to nuclear technology?

2. What impact did the U.S. and Soviet 1961–62 test series have upon the relative state of the art? What is the trend?

3. What outstanding U.S. requirements for nuclear testing exist?

4. What impact will the treaty have upon U.S. ability to fulfill these requirements?

5. What direct and indirect constraints will the treaty impose upon the United States?

6. What military or technological advantages might accrue to the United States as a result of the treaty?

7. What military or technological advantages might accrue to the Soviet Union as a result of the treaty?

8. Can the United States afford a position of parity with the Soviet Union in nuclear technology?

9. How will the treaty affect United States strategic planning?

10. What immediate risks to the national security attend the treaty?

11. Are the risks and disadvantages to the treaty manageable or under control?

12. Will the effective implementation of the safeguards recommended by the Joint Chiefs of Staff ameliorate any risks the treaty may portend?

13. Are United States and Soviet political interests and goals in conflict?

14. What impact might the treaty have on United States-Soviet areas of tension?

15. How might the treaty further Soviet political goals?

16. How might the treaty further United States political goals?

17. What political advantages or disadvantages might accrue to the United States as a result of the treaty?

18. What political advantages or disadvantages might accrue to the Soviet Union as a result of the treaty?

The answers to most of these questions, especially those concerned with military and technological matters, obviously require facts and judgments that can be provided only by military, political, and technical officials and experts who are, or recently have been, directly involved in nuclear research, the development of weapons systems, strategic planning, military operations, and intelligence. Outside of the executive branch of the United States government only Congress has access to most of these key persons and the pertinent security information they generate and control. Congress has the authority to hold hearings and conduct investigations of the activities of the executive branch at its pleasure; it can call as witnesses such government officials and other persons as it deems advisable; it has access to all pertinent classified information (except privileged communications, such as the Kennedy-Khrushchev correspondence of December, 1962); it is organized into committees and subcommittees, which permit the development of specialized areas of expertise; it has skilled and specialized assistance available in the form of personal and committee staffs; and it can release the results of its hearings and investigations to the public in the form of verbatim records of hearings, reports, and press releases.

In the case of the Test Ban Treaty, two committees of the Senate conducted separate inquiries into its implications and each published both a report on the treaty[5] and a verbatim record of its hearings. As a result of the work of these two committees, an independent, unclassified analysis of the military, technological, and political implications of the Test Ban Treaty is now possible, based upon essentially the same body of information that was available to the decision-makers in the executive branch. Because the hearings and reports of these two Senate committees provide a large and essential part of the information for this study, and, further, because one committee endorsed the treaty while the other warned against its military implications, it will be useful to discuss the organization and conduct of the two hearings briefly, with emphasis on their differences.

In connection with the process of treaty ratification, the Senate referred the treaty to the Foreign Relations Committee, which held hearings from August 12 to August 27, 1963. The Preparedness Investigating Subcommittee of the Senate Armed Services Committee became involved when it launched its investigation of arms control proposals on September 17, 1962. The Chairman of the subcommittee explained the *raison d'être* of the hearings as follows:

> The Preparedness Investigating Subcommittee, as the representative of the Committee on Armed Services, is vitally concerned with proposals which have as their purpose the limitations, control, reduction, or elimination of armed forces

---

[5] The Foreign Relations Committee published its report, entitled *The Nuclear Test Ban Treaty,* on September 3, 1963. The Preparedness Investigating Subcommittee published its report, entitled *Military Implications of the Proposed Limited Nuclear Test Ban Treaty,* on September 9, 1963.

and armaments. Our national security is inseparably entwined with all such proposals. We believe, therefore, that these proposals and policies underlying them should be subjected to scrutiny from a military point of view as well as from the standpoint of foreign policy. This is our main purpose in this inquiry.[6]

After three days of hearings in September, 1962, the subcommittee suspended its work on this subject until May 15, 1963, when it initiated an extensive inquiry into current U.S. proposals for a test ban treaty that continued through August 27, 1963. In his opening statement on May 15, the Chairman, Senator John Stennis, said: "It is both desirable and necessary that the Senate should have available to it essentially the same body of evidence as is available to the executive branch in formulating our policy."[7] In sharp contrast to this statement, the Chairman of the Foreign Relations Committee, Senator J. W. Fulbright, made no opening statement, and, in fact, had come out in favor of the treaty before he initiated the hearings.[8] Apparently he had made up his mind to support the treaty even before he organized and conducted his hearings. Further, he objected to the Preparedness Investigating Subcommittee's holding hearings on the Test Ban Treaty. During the Senate debate on the treaty he said:

> I say that it is most unusual for a subcommittee of the Armed Services Committee to take up a treaty and hold hearings on it. I know of no precedent whatever in the history of

---

[6] U.S. Congress, Senate Committee on Armed Services, Preparedness Investigating Subcommittee, *Hearings on Arms Control and Disarmament,* 87th Cong., 2d sess., 1962, p. 1.

[7] U.S. Congress, Senate, Committee on Armed Services, Preparedness Investigating Subcommittee, *Hearings on Military Aspects and Implications of Nuclear Test Ban Proposals and Related Matters,* 88th Cong., 1st Sess., 1963, p. 3. Hereafter cited as *Preparedness Investigating Subcommittee Hearings.*

[8] *Congressional Record, op. cit.,* September 16, 1963, p. 16177.

the Senate, since I have been a Senator, for a subcommittee of another committee to presume to take up a treaty in the first place.[9]

The differing attitudes of the chairmen of the two committees were reflected in the conduct and orientation of their investigations. The hearings of the Foreign Relations Committee, which supported the treaty, were relatively superficial and solicited very little classified information, but were printed, released, and distributed in time to be a major factor in the Senate debate of the treaty. The hearings of the Preparedness Investigating Subcommittee, which warned against the military implications of the treaty, consisted almost entirely of classified information and were held up by Department of Defense declassification proceedings until March 22, 1964, six months after the Senate had given its advice and consent to the treaty. The effect of this procedural delay was that during the heated debate and the Senate vote on the treaty only a small part of the voluminous information collected by the Preparedness Investigating Subcommittee was available to the Senate and the public; not until these hearings were released was enough information available to determine the military, technological, and political implications of the treaty reasonably and objectively.

Although the two hearings were both concerned with the same subject and essentially the same problem, their scope and depth were quite different. Both are essential to this study; however, the Preparedness Investigating Subcommittee hearings contain much more essential primary source material. The subcommittee explored the military and technological aspects of the treaty in great depth, whereas the Foreign Relations Committee's treatment of these aspects was somewhat superficial. The Preparedness Investigating Subcommittee, however, did not touch on the purely political

[9] *Ibid.,* September 9, 1963, p. 15637.

aspects of the treaty, which were more thoroughly explored by the Foreign Relations Committee.

The Foreign Relations Committee heard a total of forty-three witnesses, sixteen of whom are considered key to this study. The Preparedness Investigating Subcommittee called nineteen principal witnesses;[10] eighteen of them are key to this study. Of the total of fifty-six witnesses heard by the two committees, only twenty-six are considered primary sources of essential information for the purposes of this study, and eighteen of these testified before the Preparedness Investigating Subcommittee.[11]

Of the twenty-six key witnesses, eight testified before both committees; the Foreign Relations Committee heard eight that the Preparedness Investigating Subcommittee did not call, and the Preparedness Investigating Subcommittee called ten that the Foreign Relations Committee did not hear.[12] Secretary of Defense Robert S. McNamara was requested to testify before both committees, but he indicated in a letter to Chairman Stennis of the Preparedness Investigating Subcommittee that he would rather not testify before that committee, and the Chairman did not insist.[13] Of the remaining seven key witnesses heard by the Foreign Relations Committee but not by the Preparedness Investigating Subcommittee, three (Secretary of State Dean Rusk, Dr. Marshall D. Shulman, and Dr. Robert Strausz-Hupé) were political witnesses and thus did not come within the scope of the subcommittee's inquiry. On the other hand, nine of the ten key witnesses called by the subcommittee but not by the Foreign Relations Committee gave testimony essential to a thorough understanding of the military and technological

---

10 Some principal witnesses were accompanied by aides who also entered into the colloquy.

11 *See* Appendix I, "Test Ban Treaty Principal Witnesses."

12 *Ibid.*

13 *Congressional Record, op. cit.,* September 13, p. 16111.

implications of the treaty. As Senator Russell B. Long of the Foreign Relations Committee said during the Senate debate on the treaty: "At the time the Foreign Relations Committee met [to report the treaty] it did not have available to it the information that was presented to the Preparedness Investigating Subcommittee of the Committee on Armed Services."[14]

The above discussion and a review of Appendix I, "Test Ban Treaty Principal Witnesses," show that the Foreign Relations Committee did not explore the military and technological implications of the treaty as thoroughly as the Preparedness Investigating Subcommittee did, in part because it did not call a number of very important witnesses. Beyond this, however, there were three other weaknesses in the Foreign Relations hearings as compared with those of the Preparedness Investigating Subcommittee.

First, the Foreign Relations Committee heard testimony on eleven days and held twenty-one sessions, while the Preparedness Investigating Subcommittee held hearings on nineteen days for a total of twenty-nine sessions. Clearly, then, the Preparedness Investigating Subcommittee spent more time on its investigation and was able to devote much more time to each key witness because its time was not consumed by a large number of less important witnesses.

Second, the Foreign Relations Committee held only two executive sessions, where classified information could be heard, whereas all twenty-nine of the Preparedness Investigating Subcommittee's sessions were closed. Obviously it is extremely difficult, if not impossible, to probe deeply into the military and technological implications of the treaty and at the same time avoid military, technical, and intelligence secrets. Dr. Edward Teller, for example, pleaded with the Chairman of the Foreign Relations Committee to be per-

---

[14] *Ibid.,* September 20, 1963, p. 16733.

mitted to testify in executive session and thus provide them with pertinent classified information, but to no avail; the Chairman of the committee refused to recall him in executive session.[15] The result of this rushed, open-session procedure was that military and technical witnesses were severely limited in what they could say, being unable to reveal or discuss classified information.

Third, the Preparedness Investigating Subcommittee's hearings were more easily manageable than the Foreign Relations Committee's hearings. The Foreign Relations Committee invited the Armed Services Committee and the Senate members of the Joint Committee on Atomic Energy to sit with them, resulting in a maximum of thirty-eight Senators questioning forty-three witnesses. Because the examining panel was so large and the witnesses so numerous, the Chairman restricted each Senator to ten minutes of questioning time.[16] This proved to be a severe restriction; it inhibited the development of a systematic and orderly pattern of colloquy and the pursuit of a question in depth. The Preparedness Investigating Subcommittee was not burdened with an excessively large panel because it consisted of only seven members, all of whom, by virtue of their specialized experience on the subcommittee, were familiar with the military and technical problems involved.[17] Chairman Stennis did not find it necessary to limit the Senators' time, and this permitted each member to develop a line of questioning to its conclusion. The quality and thoroughness of the subcommittee's investigation were further enhanced through the services of a highly qualified special consultant, Russell Fee, who helped plan and organize the hearings and actively participated in the colloquy, thus insuring that each witness was

---

[15] *Foreign Relations Committee Hearings, op. cit.,* pp. 444, 449, 462.

[16] *See* Appendix II, "Foreign Relations Committee Hearings."

[17] *See* Appendix III, "Preparedness Investigating Subcommittee Hearings."

utilized to the maximum and that the information sought was systematically developed in accordance with a carefully laid plan.

In short, while both hearings are needed to analyze the treaty effectively, the primary value of the Foreign Relations Committee's hearings is in the field of political implications, while the hearings of the Preparedness Investigating Subcommittee are essential to any thorough analysis of the military and technological implications of the treaty. Without the work of the Preparedness Investigating Subcommittee, a study of this nature would be impossible.

Finally, it should be noted that the most important by-product of the Senate's inquiries into the treaty, the formalization of the safeguards recommended by the Joint Chiefs of Staff, was accomplished, not by the Foreign Relations Committee, but by the Preparedness Investigating Subcommittee,[18] whose hearings probably had little effect on the Senate vote on the treaty.

---

[18] *See* Chapter VII, "The Safeguards."

chapter 2

HISTORICAL BACKGROUND

The Test Ban Treaty, commonly known as the Moscow Treaty, was the first significant arms control treaty to come out of seventeen years of negotiation between the Western Allies and the Soviet Union. Efforts to limit or prohibit the testing of nuclear weapons through international agreement began in 1946, when the United Nations General Assembly adopted a resolution setting up a U.N. Atomic Energy Commission to prepare specific proposals for the purpose of controlling atomic energy. At the first meeting of this commission, on June 14, 1946, Bernard Baruch presented the United States plan for an International Atomic Development Authority, to which would be entrusted all phases of the development and use of atomic energy. Under this plan the United States would have given up all its knowledge and facilities concerning atomic energy to international control under safeguards designed to prevent any nation from developing or employing atomic energy independently. While the United Nations approved the plan, the Soviet Union rejected it, thus making it impossible of execution.

Subsequently the Soviet Union and the United States alternated in submitting proposals for the control or abolition of atomic weapons. These proposals came to naught, because the United States could not accept Soviet proposals, which would leave them without either an atomic deterrent or an inspection system to protect the Free World, especially Europe, from Soviet aggression. On the other hand, the Soviet Union insisted that the United States give up its nuclear deterrent, but refused to agree to any meaningful inspection system.

Meanwhile, behind the facade of negotiations, the Soviet

13

Union undertook a maximum effort to break the American nuclear monopoly and achieve its own nuclear capability. The Soviets' rate of progress completely surprised the West; their first atomic device was tested in 1949, and their first hydrogen bomb in 1953. From this point on, the Soviet Union rapidly developed its nuclear strike capability while on the diplomatic level it continued to propose arms control measures that, if accepted, would have crippled Western nuclear power.

In August, 1957, in an attempt to break the deadlock, the United States presented a package proposal to the United Nations Disarmament Commission calling for the cessation of nuclear weapons testing and production, the reduction of nuclear weapons stockpiles through conversion of fissionable materials to peaceful uses, and certain limitations on conventional arms and forces. This proposal was rejected by the Soviet Union, whereupon the United States announced a resumption of nuclear testing beginning in the spring of 1958.

On March 31, 1958, just after the Soviet Union had completed a nuclear test series and just before the United States commenced its test series, the Soviet Union announced that it was unilaterally suspending further testing, with the reservation that it might resume testing if the United States and the United Kingdom did not join in the suspension.

The United States did not permit this offer to deter the scheduled test series, but on August 22 the United States and Great Britain announced that they would suspend testing for one year, commencing October 31, 1958, and for additional one-year periods, provided the Soviet Union would also desist from testing and would agree to join the United States and Great Britain in negotiations for the suspension of nuclear tests and the establishment of an international control system. The control system was to be based upon the report of a conference of technical experts who met in

Geneva from July 1 to August 21, 1958. The Soviet Union agreed to the negotiations, but conducted two nuclear tests after the October 31 deadline, and the Western powers chose to disregard these tests.

During these negotiations the United States, for the first time, agreed to separate the consideration of prohibiting nuclear testing from broader disarmament proposals. This concession came to naught, and the negotiations were soon deadlocked over the inspection issue. The Soviet Union adamantly refused to accept any meaningful inspection system, while the Western powers insisted upon reasonable safeguards; hence no progress was made.

On April 13, 1959, the United States, with the concurrence of Great Britain, proposed that, as a first step toward a comprehensive test ban treaty, an agreement be concluded to ban only atmospheric and underwater testing, and thus avoid the troublesome issue of detecting underground and space tests. Again the Soviet Union rejected the proposal.

The following year, on February 11, 1960, the United States proposed an uninspected partial test ban, this time suggesting that all nuclear testing in the atmosphere, underwater, in space, and underground—except for small explosions—be banned. The Soviet Union objected to the exception and rejected the proposal.

During the next three years negotiations proceeded at a slow and fruitless pace, interrupted by several crises that offered the United States adequate justification for breaking off negotiations. First, Soviet Premier Khrushchev scuttled the May, 1960, summit conference by directing a tirade of abuse at President Eisenhower over the U-2 incident. He further announced that he would have no more dealings with the Eisenhower administration and would wait until the following year, when a new administration would be inaugurated, to deal with the United States. Second, the Berlin crisis of the summer of 1961 strained relations severely, and this was followed on September 1 by the unannounced Soviet abrogation of the moratorium. Then came the Cuban crisis of October, 1962, when the United States discovered at the last moment that the Soviet Union had surreptitiously introduced medium-range ballistic missiles armed with nuclear warheads into that island.

In spite of these provocations, the United States persisted in its pursuit of a test ban treaty. In August, 1962, in the middle of the second post-moratorium Soviet test series, the United States and the United Kingdom tabled two important treaties: one proposed a ban on all nuclear testing, safeguarded by a system of internationally supervised control posts and on-site inspections; the other called for the uninspected prohibition of testing in all environments except underground. The latter proposal was very similar to the Moscow Treaty of 1963. The Soviet Union flatly rejected both proposals; however, in December, 1962, two months after the Cuban crisis and *a few days after completion of the Soviet test series*, Premier Khrushchev indicated in a letter to President Kennedy that the Soviet Union might accept a test ban agreement on the basis of two or three inspections a year on Soviet territory plus a few unmanned seismic stations. While this was not acceptable to the United States, it provided some incentive to keep the test ban talks alive, because it seemed to indicate the Soviet Union's acceptance of the principle of on-site inspection.

Negotiations were resumed on January 22, 1963, by representatives of the United States, Great Britain, and the Soviet Union, who had for their guidance the exchange of letters between Premier Khrushchev and President Kennedy.[1]

The negotiations were promptly deadlocked over the on-

---

[1] *Congressional Record* (daily edition), 88th Cong., 1st Sess., January 21, 1963, pp. 657–59. The exchange of letters took place in December, 1962, less than two months after the Cuban crisis.

site inspection issue, and in an attempt to get past this hurdle, President Kennedy, on January 26, 1963, ordered a suspension of the United States underground test series then underway.[2] This action succeeded in interrupting the U.S. test program, but failed to mollify the Soviets, who countered with a proposal to drop the three-power talks and return the negotiations to the Eighteen Nation Disarmament Committee, which was scheduled to reconvene in Geneva on February 12, 1963.

In commenting on the suspension of the negotiations, Secretary of State Rusk said:

> The basic position of the Soviet Union seems to be that the national systems, so-called, are adequate to determine whether surreptitious underground tests are in fact being carried out. Now from the point of view of the Soviet Union, thinking about the possibility of underground tests in the United States, this may well be so, because of the open nature of our society, the enormous difficulty which we would have in conducting secret underground tests, and the ready availability of information may give them confidence that, if there is a test ban treaty, they would know in fact, we were conducting tests.

> But our situation is different, because we are concerned about the possibility of secret tests in a vast area, much of it sparsely populated, inhabited by a closed society, where the ordinary means of information about what is going on in the country are simply not available. Therefore to us the idea of on-site inspection is not simply a political question involving the acceptance of on-site inspection in principle, but is the practical problem of establishing arrangements which in fact do provide assurance that agreements are being complied with.[3]

---

[2] *Washington Post,* January 27, 1963.
[3] "News Conference Remarks by Secretary of State Rusk," *Department of State Bulletin,* February 18, 1963, pp. 235–36.

He then confirmed that the United States was canceling its suspension of underground testing.[4]

The Eighteen Nation talks soon came to an impasse over the inspection issue, although the United States reduced its security requirements to seven yearly inspections. The Soviet Union refused to budge from its offer of from two to three. Then on February 19 a rumor was widely circulated in Congress that the United States might again lower the number of inspections it demanded. In this connection there had been a number of Senators who questioned the wisdom of suspending testing and were especially concerned about the steady lowering of United States requirements for on-site inspections. The speech made by Senator Thomas J. Dodd (D., Conn.) on the Senate floor on February 21, 1963, was illustrative of that feeling.[5] He enumerated the progressive concessions made by the United States during the course of the test ban negotiations and warned that "the road of appeasement or concessions . . . is not the road to peace but the road to slavery, the road to a permanent and unending war upon everything in which we believe."[6]

Attempts to break the impasse in the negotiations at Geneva proved fruitless, and United States officials were pessimistic that any agreement could be reached. Then on May 27 Senators Dodd and Humphrey, together with thirty-two of their colleagues, offered a resolution urging the government to propose a partial test ban treaty and suggesting that if the Soviet Union rejected the offer, the United States should unilaterally suspend atmospheric and underwater nuclear testing.[7]

President Kennedy's speech at American University June

[4] *Ibid.*, p. 237.
[5] *Congressional Record, op. cit.*, February 21, 1963, pp. 2660–2701.
[6] *Ibid.*, p. 2671.
[7] Senate Resolution 148, 88th Cong., 1st Sess., May 27, 1963, *Congressional Record, op. cit.*, May 27, 1963, p. 8948.

10 seemed to be a direct follow-up of the Senators' suggestion, or perhaps the Senate resolution had been inspired by the White House. In any event, the President announced that the United States, Great Britain, and the Soviet Union would soon begin a new round of high-level talks in Moscow, "looking toward early agreement on a comprehensive test ban treaty," and that the United States would refrain from atmospheric testing so long as other nations did not test. He said that a test ban would help check "one of the greatest hazards which man faces in 1963, the further spread of nuclear weapons." He also called upon the American public to "re-examine our attitude toward the Soviet Union."[8]

On the same day, British Labor party leader Harold Wilson conferred in Moscow with Soviet Premier Khrushchev for more than three hours, and subsequently announced at a press conference that "the immediate prospects for a full test ban agreement based on inspection are not very hopeful." He added, however, that "the possibility of a test ban confined to atmospheric tests, space and underwater tests . . . seems to offer more hope of agreement."[9]

On June 14 Premier Khrushchev, in commenting upon President Kennedy's June 10 speech, said that it made a "favorable impression." With regard to a nuclear test ban treaty, he said:

We are ready to sign an agreement on the discontinuance of all nuclear tests even today. We agreed to a meeting between the representatives of the three powers in Moscow to try once again to reach an agreement on this question. But the success of this meeting will depend upon the luggage the United States and British representatives take with them to our country.[10]

---

[8] "The Strategy of Peace," *Department of State Bulletin*, July 1, 1963, pp. 2–6.
[9] *New York Times,* June 11, 1963.
[10] *Ibid.,* June 15, 1963.

Then on July 2, in an address to a rally in Berlin, Khrushchev announced that the Soviet Union would be willing to sign a treaty banning nuclear weapons tests in the atmosphere, underwater, and in space, but tied such a treaty to a nonaggression treaty between the NATO powers and the Warsaw Treaty states.[11] The next day both Washington and London released announcements to the effect that they would be willing to accept a partial test ban treaty, and at long last the stage seemed set for agreement.

The three-power talks opened in Moscow on Monday, July 15. The American delegation was headed by W. Averell Harriman, Under-Secretary of State for Political Affairs; the British delegation by Viscount Hailsham, Minister of Science; and the Soviet delegation at the first session by Premier Khrushchev, and subsequently by Foreign Minister Andrei Gromyko. The conference progressed rapidly, and by the following Saturday had reached tentative agreement on a treaty that would ban nuclear testing in the atmosphere, in space, and underwater. The draft treaty was initialed by the chief delegates of each of the three powers on the evening of July 25, 1963. On August 5 the treaty was formally signed in Moscow by Secretary of State Rusk, British Secretary of State for Foreign Affairs Lord Home, and Soviet Foreign Minister Gromyko. The American delegation was accompanied by six senators: Fulbright, Sparkman, Humphrey and Aiken of the Foreign Relations Committee; Saltonstall of the Armed Services Committee; and Pastore of the Joint Committee on Atomic Energy.

President Kennedy transmitted the treaty to the Senate on August 8, where it was referred to the Foreign Relations Committee as "Executive M, 88th Congress, 1st Session." The Foreign Relations Committee conducted hearings on the

---

[11] "Statement by Premier Khrushchev in Berlin, July 2, 1963," *Current Digest of the Soviet Press,* July 31, 1963, pp. 8–9.

treaty from August 12 to August 27, and reported it out favorably on September 3 by a vote of sixteen to one. Senator Russell B. Long (D., La.) was the sole dissenter. The Senate Armed Services Committee held closed hearings on the military implications of the treaty from August 1 to August 27, and rendered an unfavorable report on September 9. The Senate debate of the treaty was initiated on the same day and continued until September 24, when the Senate approved ratification by a vote of eighty to nineteen. On the same day the African Republic of Niger signed the treaty, the one hundred and second nation to do so. The treaty was signed by President Kennedy on October 7, and on October 10 the ratification was duly certified in Moscow, London, and Washington, thus entering the treaty into force.

Principal Provisions of the Treaty[12]

In the preamble to the treaty its principal aim is declared to be "general and complete disarmament under strict international control," and "the discontinuance of all test explosions of nuclear weapons for all time."

Under Article I, each signatory power undertakes to refrain from nuclear weapons test explosions or any other explosions in the atmosphere, outer space, or underwater at any place under its jurisdiction or control. Underground testing is not prohibited unless it releases radioactive debris that travels beyond the borders of the State under whose jurisdiction the explosion is conducted. The parties to the treaty also agree to refrain from causing, encouraging, or participating in the carrying out of any nuclear explosion anywhere in the prohibited environments.

---

[12] For the complete text of the treaty, see Appendix IV, "The Nuclear Test Ban Treaty."

Article II provides machinery for subsequent amendment of the treaty. Any party to the treaty may propose amendments, and if one-third or more of the parties so desire, the depository governments are obliged to convene a conference to consider such amendments. An amendment can be made by a majority vote of all the parties to the treaty, including *all* the votes of the original three parties (United States, United Kingdom, and U.S.S.R.). Under this provision, then, any one of the original parties may veto any proposed amendment.

Article III provides that the treaty shall be open to all States for signature, and that any State can accede to it after it enters into force.[13]

Under Article IV, the treaty is of unlimited duration. Any party, however, can withdraw upon three-months' notice to all of the other parties if it decides that its national interests are jeopardized by extraordinary events relating to the subject matter of the treaty.

---

[13] By the time the Senate ratified the treaty, 102 nations had become signatories.

chapter 3

THE STATE OF THE ART IN THE UNITED STATES AND THE SOVIET UNION

In his message transmitting the Test Ban Treaty to the Senate, President Kennedy said: "It [the treaty] grows out of the proposal made by President Eisenhower in 1959. . . . Nothing has happened since then to alter its importance to our security." He went on to say that the post-moratorium test series conducted by the United States and the Soviet Union "have not resulted in any substantial alteration of the strategic balance."[1] This statement deserves serious consideration.

In the first place, the effect of the 1961–62 test series on the relative state of the art in the United States and the Soviet Union should not be overlooked. One wonders, in light of the President's statement, whether he had been thoroughly briefed on the scope, magnitude, orientation, and relationship to future developments of the two Soviet test series. While the United States was decisively ahead in nuclear technology, as it was in 1958, a nuclear test ban was clearly to its advantage, but the Soviet Union would have no part of it. But if a condition of parity or, even worse, Soviet superiority, existed as a result of the 1961–62 test series, then a test ban treaty would be a different matter.

Second, the President was correct in saying that the post-moratorium test series had not resulted in any substantial alteration of the strategic balance. The reason it had not however, is because a test series immediately affects only the level or quality of technology, and this cannot be trans

---

[1] "Text of President Kennedy's Treaty Message to the Senate," *Co gressional Quarterly Weekly Report,* August 16, 1963, p. 1457.

formed into weapons systems in less than six to eight years, and it is weapons systems that do affect the strategic balance. The United States is superior in strategic power today because it was superior in technology six to eight years ago, and if that superiority disappeared with the 1961–62 test series, strategic superiority may well disappear six to eight years in the future.

It is interesting to note that while the decisions affecting nuclear technology a president makes will probably not affect the strategic power of the nation during his term of office, they may largely determine the degree of strategic superiority—or inferiority—available to his successor. This is an ironic fact of life in the nuclear age; the decisions made by President Eisenhower gave President Kennedy the opportunity to build superior weapons systems, and the decisions President Kennedy made may determine whether his successor and his successor's successor have the opportunity to build superior strategic systems to defend the nation. If President Kennedy made a mistake in the Test Ban Treaty his administration would not suffer for it, but future presidents might be severely restricted by the decision. For this reason the Soviet and American test series and the resultant state of the art in the United States and the Soviet Union must be carefully examined with an eye to the future.

The 1961–62 Test Series

The two hearings on the Test Ban Treaty before the Senate brought out the fact that through its massive 1961–62 test series, the Soviet Union made a quantum jump in nuclear technology while the United States lagged far behind. Dr. John Foster, Director of the Lawrence Radiation Laboratory, told the Foreign Relations Committee that

the discouraging point is that currently, from their recent atmospheric series and from our recent atmospheric series, I see a very high rate of progress in the Soviet Union. If this were to continue . . . it would be to the detriment of the United States.[2]

Dr. Norris E. Bradbury, Director of the Los Alamos Laboratory, felt that through these test series the Soviet Union had come from a position far behind the United States to one of rough parity, while Dr. Edward Teller declared that the Soviets were now ahead. General Twining, who was chairman of the group of technical experts that analyzed the Soviet test series and rendered a top-secret report to the Air Force and the Department of Defense, told the Preparedness Investigating Subcommittee:

> In April, 1959, when the Soviet proposal to suspend nuclear tests was rejected, it was generally agreed that the United States held a substantial lead in nuclear technology. . . . When the United States signed the limited test ban treaty this lead had essentially disappeared, as a result of the Soviet test series which began in September 1961 and ended in December 1962.[3]

He said that in his judgment this situation did "bear significantly, even dangerously, upon our power position relative to the Soviet Union."[4]

In retrospect, it appears that the 1958–61 moratorium was a Soviet trap baited with nothing more than hope; yet the political leaders of the United States, with Soviet encouragement, came to believe that their hopes were realities.

United States intelligence failed to give warning of the Soviet preparations for testing; official political judgment

---

[2] *Foreign Relations Committee Hearings, op. cit.,* pp. 619–20.
[3] *Preparedness Investigating Subcommittee Hearings, op. cit.,* p. 970.
[4] *Ibid.*

erred in assessing Soviet intentions; and for unknown and unexplained reasons a prudent posture of readiness was not maintained, despite the pleas and warnings of the military establishment and the Atomic Energy Commission laboratories.

In order to conduct the massive, well-organized, and objectively oriented test series they did, the Soviets probably started preparations soon after the moratorium was declared, while the ruse lulled the political leadership of the United States into inactivity and euphoric dreams of détente and security through arms control. General Twining, who probably studied the Soviet test series more thoroughly than anyone else in the United States, said:

> They used the period of the moratorium as a springboard for an extensive new series of tests, and, put another way, they lost nothing by the moratorium because they were busy planning the results of the 1958 tests.
>
> Then, in 1961, they had finished their laboratory work and developed weapons and identified new areas requiring testing. In other words, when they were good and ready, they broke the moratorium and resumed testing, and I mean resumed testing right now, with no delays. They had this well planned.
>
> In the meantime, we all but allowed our testing capability to go to seed![5]

To put the picture in proper perspective it is necessary to examine and compare the massive Soviet series with the meager United States tests. The Soviets conducted two series of tests. The first started September 1, 1961, and continued through the fall, while the second started in July, 1962, and ended in December of the same year. They conducted about one hundred tests in the atmosphere, an unknown but prob-

---

[5] *Ibid.*, p. 972.

ably small number underground, and several at very high altitudes. The resumption of testing caught the United States by complete surprise and totally unprepared. The United States started off with a few relatively meaningless underground tests in September, mainly for psychological reasons, but was unable to resume atmospheric testing of any kind until April 25, 1962. In 1962 about sixty underground and twenty-eight atmospheric tests were conducted. In 1963 the United States conducted another thirty underground tests prior to the Test Ban Treaty, but no atmospheric tests whatsoever.

The United States series did not match the Soviet series in either magnitude or scope. The Soviets conducted weapons development tests from the very small range up to the largest test ever conducted, about sixty megatons. They also conducted proof tests, weapons systems tests, effects tests, and tests with missiles and radar. In their two test series they conducted more tests above one megaton than the United States had made in its entire history.[6] The Soviet Union detonated about three hundred megatons, while the United States series amounted to only about one-tenth of that.[7] The United States series was mostly in the low yield spectrum and predominately of the weapons development type, while the Soviet series ranged across the entire yield spectrum.

The Soviet series seemed directed toward specific systems and effects problems, while the United States series was described by Dr. John Foster as "some very interesting scientific probes into the phenomenology of nuclear effects."[8] General Power, Commander-in-Chief of the Strategic Air Command, told the Preparedness Investigating Subcommittee that in the United States test series "one of the most im-

---

6 *Ibid.*, p. 801.
7 *Ibid.*, p. 473. *See also* p. 353.
8 *Foreign Relations Committee Hearings, op. cit.*, p. 623.

portant things we discovered is the great void in our knowledge,"[9] while General Le May described the series as "hastily thrown together, and not very well thought out."[10] There can be no doubt that the 1961–62 test series seriously degraded the United States position relative to the Soviet Union and was a severe blow to United States prestige.

How did it happen that the Soviet Union was able to make such a leap in technology while the United States was unable to keep pace? The American deficiency was not the result of any scientific or technical inferiority vis à vis the Soviet Union, but rather lies in the arena of political decisions. There were two reasons for the poor American showing: first, the Department of Defense and the Atomic Energy Commission had been ordered to cease all preparations for testing and, as a consequence, their capability was in a state of decay; and second, the technicians were not authorized by their political superiors to conduct even those experiments they were capable of executing. In other words, at the highest political level, the United States had established a policy of self-abnegation. The readiness to test posture had decayed to such an extent that Dr. John Foster estimated that it would take two years of maximum effort "to be able to reach the rate of operations demonstrated by the Soviets."[11] Even Secretary of Defense McNamara admitted: "I think that we were reasonably well prepared for the tests we conducted, but we weren't prepared for the tests we didn't conduct. *Those were the tests that were important.*"[12]

The laboratories and the test facilities were not prepared to launch a test series primarily because they had been ordered not to and were denied the means needed to. In January, 1960, the Secretary of Defense ordered all preparations

---

[9] *Preparedness Investigating Subcommittee Hearings, op. cit.,* p. 801.
[10] *Ibid.,* p. 357.
[11] *Foreign Relations Committee Hearings, op. cit.,* p. 621.
[12] *Ibid.,* p. 122 (emphasis supplied).

for testing to cease. As a result, the Air Force Special Weapons Center for Nuclear Testing dwindled from a work force of one thousand men to only fourteen as of September 1, 1961.[13] The Nevada testing grounds were not maintained and had to be rebuilt to sustain resumed testing. Activity at Eniwetok was first curtailed and then abandoned altogether. The joint task force for nuclear testing was disbanded. Dr. Leland J. Haworth of the Atomic Energy Commission reported to the Preparedness Investigating Subcommittee:

> As the moratorium continued and plans and programs were revised, delayed, reduced, and often canceled, all of the activities bearing on testing capability began to suffer from a loss of personnel, often the most competent of them.[14]

Laboratory capabilities evaporated and all sense of urgency or pride of accomplishment disappeared. Dr. John Foster, Director of Lawrence Radiation Laboratory, testified:

> Despite the 60 odd major letters and teletypes exchanged between the laboratory and the Atomic Energy Commission, it was not possible to get authorized the degree of readiness, preparation of facilities, and so on which the laboratory desired. And finally, when we did go back to test, we started very slowly because our skills had decayed.[15]

The decay of skills, abandonment of test grounds, disbanding of organizations, and lack of preparations drastically limited the crash program that the Soviet breach of the moratorium forced upon the United States. There had been little advance planning or preparation for badly needed effects tests, so little could be done in this field, and there were at least three failures in those tests that were attempted.[16] Col.

---

[13] *Preparedness Investigating Subcommittee Hearings, op. cit.,* p. 387.
[14] *Ibid.,* p. 259.
[15] *Ibid.,* p. 396.
[16] *Ibid.,* p. 260.

Roy J. Clinton of the Defense Atomic Support Agency told the Preparedness Investigating Subcommittee:

> It was well recognized by the scientific Community that a large yield burst would be the most useful experiment for the study of these effects—vulnerability of hardened sites to blast and shock effects—[deleted] but this was not possible on the short time scale.[17]

Tests in the high yield range were also impossible because of lack of preparation and the short time scale. No matter how urgent the need for effects tests and high yield tests might have been, under the circumstances, they simply could not be accomplished.

Even though the testing capability was severely hampered by decay of skills, abandonment of facilities, loss of personnel, and lack of planning and preparation, it was further restricted by policy decisions made at the highest level of government. The laboratories and the military establishment proposed many important tests that were capable of execution, only to be denied authority to go ahead. Dr. Bradbury told the Preparedness Investigating Subcommittee that "the ones for which we did not get approval were probably the ones which we put the greatest emphasis on."[18] Dr. Foster testified that "during the last year, the laboratories have been under severe nontechnical restrictions."[19] In response to Senator Humphrey's question as to why we did not test more in 1961 and 1962, Dr. Teller replied:

> Because it was the judgment of the administration that popular opinion would not tolerate more. . . . We wanted to test more. . . . We had plenty of things we wanted to look at, and we were limited because we were told from the time that the decision is made to the time the test is finished a minimum

---

17 *Ibid.*, p. 201.
18 *Ibid.*, p. 517.
19 *Ibid.*, p. 636.

period must elapse. It is one of the most serious limitations under which we labored.[20]

General Le May testified that the Air Force wanted to test-fire an Atlas missile with a warhead to test missile reliability and was refused authority to do so.[21] He further warned:

> Our weapons development testing continues to be hampered by the arbitrary limits being proposed which could place us in a position so far behind in nuclear technology that the United States might not be able to recover.[22]

So while the Soviet Union used the device of a moratorium to conceal preparations for the world's largest, most extensive, and best-planned search for nuclear technology, United States political leadership appeared to be reluctant to permit its scientific and military community to keep pace. The result, of course, had an impact on the comparative levels of technology, and this in turn will have an impact on future strategic superiority because today's technology is the backbone of tomorrow's weapons systems. The tremendous difference between the quality and scope of the Soviet and American test series in 1961 and 1962 has grave implications, not only for the future strategic balance of power, but also for American prestige in the eyes of the world. The new comparative state of the art between the United States and the Soviet Union must now be examined. This can best be accomplished by breaking it down into its various divisions and examining each in turn.

Very High Yield Range (Twenty Megatons and Above)

In the very high yield range, from twenty megatons up, there is no doubt that the Soviets are well ahead of the United

---

[20] *Foreign Relations Committee Hearings, op. cit.,* p. 440.
[21] *Preparedness Investigating Subcommittee Hearings, op. cit.,* p. 728.
[22] *Ibid.,* p. 355.

States and this lead would be frozen by an atmospheric test ban. In this range the Soviets have conducted four times as many tests as the United States. Their largest test was sixty megatons—in October, 1961, while the largest test ever conducted by the United States was about fifteen megatons—at Eniwetok in 1953.[23] The Soviets have claimed, and United States official estimates agree that it is possible, that they have a one hundred-megaton weapon capable of missile delivery. Dr. Teller told the Preparedness Investigating Subcommittee that not only had we not made any tests comparable to the Soviet tests, "even our theoretical studies on these effects are in a rather incomplete stage."[24]

Just how important is the Soviet lead in very high yield technology? On this matter there is no general consensus. Secretary McNamara and General Taylor said that they see no need for us to experiment in this field, while General Le May, General Power, and former Chairman of the Atomic Energy Commission Willard F. Libby felt that the United States should long ago have gone into the field. Dr. Harold Brown, Director of Defense Research and Engineering, took a cautious middle ground and stated, "The actual military worth of 100 megaton weapons to the United States is not clear. . . ."[25]

While the United States has done nothing in the field, there has never been agreement at the decision-making level that this was the proper course. The debate over very high yield weapons has raged in the Department of Defense and the Atomic Energy Commission since 1954, and since there was no agreement, nothing was done until shortly before the Test Ban Treaty was signed, and then it was too late. At an undisclosed time, but probably after the Soviets broke the

---

23 *Ibid.,* p. 456.
24 *Ibid.,* p. 578.
25 *Foreign Relations Committee Hearings, op. cit.,* p. 532.

moratorium, the Air Force restated its requirement for a weapon of fifty to one hundred megatons for B-52 delivery,[26] and the Joint Chiefs of Staff concluded that they may want a very high yield weapon.[27] The Department of Defense then asked the Atomic Energy Commission to give them the specifications of what could be done in the very high yield field for both B-52 and missile delivery. The ban on atmospheric testing, of course, seriously impedes progress and precludes catching up with the Soviets; however, some progress can be made with underground testing and extensive extrapolation. The consensus of technical opinion is that, if weight is no object, without further atmospheric testing a rather crude fifty-megaton weapon could be developed, but in order to develop a better weapon atmospheric testing would be required. With respect to a very high yield weapon for Titan II delivery, Secretary McNamara said that it may be possible to develop a thirty-five-megaton weapon without further testing; however, General Betts, Director of the Military Applications Division, Atomic Energy Commission, said that this definitely could not be done.

The truth of the matter seems to be that the Soviet Union holds a commanding lead in the high yield field, and without atmospheric testing there is very little the United States can do to alleviate the situation. How important the Soviet lead is in terms of military advantage is a matter of serious disagreement, and the truth can never be known until a very high yield weapon is tested and its effects carefully analyzed. There may well be exotic effects from such a weapon, such as electromagnetic pulse, that cannot be anticipated or calculated without full-scale experimentation and that may be capable of destroying the United States retaliatory forces in their silos before a single one is fired. Without testing we simply cannot know.

---

[26] *Preparedness Investigating Subcommittee Hearings, op. cit.,* p. 355.
[27] *Foreign Relations Committee Hearings, op. cit.,* p. 577.

Intermediate Range (One–Twenty Megatons)

The state of the art in the intermediate range is often considered particularly important to the United States because early development of a high yield-to-weight ratio in this range has produced powerful and sophisticated warheads for Minuteman and Polaris missiles. It is generally felt that somewhere in this range the United States technology becomes superior to that of the Soviet Union and the margin becomes progressively greater with smaller yield. Dr. Brown felt that the crossover point was about twenty megatons, while Dr. Haworth felt that it was about ten megatons. Secretary McNamara and Dr. Seaborg declared that we have a very great advantage over the Soviets because of our advantage in this range,[28] but the Joint Chiefs of Staff, in their formal statement, said, "The U.S.S.R. is about even in the intermediate range," and Dr. Teller, Dr. Foster, and General Le May doubted that the United States held any lead at all. Dr. Foster backed his stand with hard facts and cold logic. He testified:

> Looking over the hundreds of shots that have been fired in the past, analyzing each one in detail, to the extent that we can, we find that progress is reasonably well correlated with experience.
>
> Now to date the Soviets have had several times the experience of the United States in yields above one megaton.[29]

He went on to reveal another matter, perhaps the most significant single thing uncovered by the hearings. He said: "I

---

[28] *Ibid.*, p. 152.
[29] *Preparedness Investigating Subcommittee Hearings, op. cit.*, p. 437.

think if one goes through the numbers in detail, the United States has marginal capacity against hardened sites."[30] If this is true, the McNamara counter-force strategy will be useless as a strategic deterrent when the Soviet Union has hardened its missile sites. Soviet cities would have to become the targets for the Minuteman and Polaris missiles. One can only hope that the Secretary of Defense and his staff have "gone through the numbers" at least as carefully as Dr. Foster, and have not attributed to the strategic missile force a capability it does not have.

Without nuclear testing in the atmosphere it does not appear that any substantial improvements in nuclear technology in this range can be made. Dr. Seaborg testified that "complete development of new type weapons above several megatons in yield would be very difficult, if possible at all."[31] Some improvement in yield-to-weight, cleanliness, invulnerability to environment, and fusion-to-fission ratio may be accomplished through underground testing; it would seem imperative that a vigorous and imaginative underground test program be undertaken to achieve these goals.

Submegaton Range

Below the megaton range most official and technical experts were confident that the United States is ahead of the Soviet Union in design technique, yield-to-weight ratio and diversity of weapons. There appears to be some evidence to this effect down to the hundreds of kilotons, based upon the analysis of detected tests. According to Dr. Teller, however, it is virtually certain that the United States failed to detect

---

[30] *Ibid.*
[31] *Foreign Relations Committee Hearings, op. cit.,* p. 215.

and identify many Soviet tests,[32] and so this judgment may not be very firm.

Further, the Soviets' rate of testing in this range during their 1961–62 test series indicates that they are seriously challenging the American lead. Prior to the latest Soviet test series, the United States had conducted more than twice as many tests at yields below one megaton as had been detected in the Soviet Union. By the end of 1962 this ratio had dropped sharply because the Soviet Union conducted more tests in this range in 1961 and 1962 than it had conducted in its entire program from 1949 to 1958.[33]

As for tactical nuclear weapons, it is generally believed and hoped that the United States is ahead of the Soviet Union, but there is no hard evidence one way or another, since these weapons are of such low yield that it is very difficult to obtain reliable information about them. Admiral Anderson expressed the consensus well when he said:

> We feel, let us say, a little bit proud that we have come as far as we have, and as fast as we have, in our tactical nuclear weapons.
>
> Unfortunately, it is not as easy for us to get information on the low-yield weapons which the Soviets explode as it is of the high yield weapons.
>
> Therefore, I would say that while we have this intuitive feeling that we are ahead, we can't be certain of the degree to which we are ahead. We have been surprised by the Russians before.[34]

General Le May, however, would have none of this "intuitive feeling" about the United States lead in the lower

---

[32] *Preparedness Investigating Subcommittee Hearings, op. cit.*, p. 543.

[33] U. S. Congress, Senate Armed Services Committee, Preparedness Investigating Subcommittee, *Interim Report on the Military Implications of the Proposed Limited Nuclear Test Ban Treaty*, 88th Cong., 1st Sess., September 9, 1963, p. 4.

[34] *Preparedness Investigating Subcommittee Hearings, op. cit.*, p. 331.

yields. He told the Preparedness Investigating Subcommittee:

> So I am extremely doubtful about the general consensus that we are ahead in an area where we don't know what they have been doing, and it just seems strange to me that the Russians would come up with such an elaborate test program only in the area where we found out something about it, and they may well have had that same effort all across the spectrum. If this was indeed true, then there are serious doubts in my mind whether we are ahead in the lower areas or not.[35]

Whether or not the United States is ahead in the low yield range, the important fact is that it is in this area of nuclear technology that the Test Ban Treaty will present the least impediment to progress. Yields of up to one megaton can be tested underground; therefore, if the Soviets are behind, they can catch up. Their rate of progress, momentum, and steadfastness of purpose have been much greater than those of the United States, and if this trend continues they will certainly lead across the entire spectrum of nuclear technology. Even Secretary McNamara and Dr. Harold Brown seemed to assume that sooner or later the Soviets would catch up, but argued that with the Test Ban Treaty they will advance more slowly because the United States is believed to have more experience with underground testing. Dr. Brown testified: "Although the Soviets may tend to catch up if we both test underground then almost certainly they would catch up more quickly if we were both to test in the atmosphere."[36] He believed that it would take the Soviet Union six months to a year to match our technical capabilities in underground testing. This almost fatalistic resignation on the part of the Secretary of Defense and the Director of Defense Research and Engineering may be indicative of the type of

---

[35] *Ibid.*, p. 721.
[36] *Foreign Relations Committee Hearings, op. cit.*, p. 532.

thinking behind the decisions that permitted the Soviets to make their striking relative gains over the United States in 1961–62 and that is behind the pessimistic undercurrent that ran through the testimony of witnesses such as General Le May and Dr. Foster.

There is much to be done in the field of low yield technology that can be accomplished through underground testing. There is a continuing requirement for increased economy in the use of fissile material (plutonium), for increased yield-to-weight, and for increasing militarily desirable effects and reducing undesirable effects such as fallout. Further development in the field of very small battlefield weapons of very low yield has also been requested by the Army. All this is deemed useful in increasing the flexibility of battlefield capability and can be accomplished through a vigorous underground testing program if such a program is authorized, planned, and implemented.

Nuclear Weapons Effects

All witnesses agreed that at the current state of the art in nuclear technology the greatest need for nuclear testing is in the area of weapons effects, and this information can be gained only by testing in the atmosphere. In testimony before the Preparedness Investigating Subcommittee, Dr. John Foster explained:

> The most serious void has to do with the effect that nuclear explosions has on the operation of the system, whether it is an offensive or defensive explosion or an offensive or defensive system.
>
> One can and should do a great deal of experimenting in the atmosphere with these systems to see whether or not they can function properly even without the presence of nuclear explosions.

The difficulty is, however, that since we know that nuclear explosions in the atmosphere can disrupt sky features that represent the determinants of the system, we are uncertain as to whether or not the explosions that might occur in the real situation will remove our capability.[37]

He went on to point out that as the United States margin of superiority becomes less, security depends more on knowledge of the vulnerability of both friendly and enemy forces and the enemy's estimate of friendly vulnerability. Vulnerability in turn depends upon the effects of nuclear explosions, so there is an ever-increasing need for effects testing, and this can be done only in the atmosphere. The basic question is how hard anything is to nuclear effects, be it an antiballistic missile, a reentry vehicle, a hardened silo, communications, etc., and will it function as designed in a nuclear environment. The fact that the United States has adopted a second-strike posture renders the acquisition of effects knowledge crucial, since its weapons will have to survive the effects of a first strike and then penetrate enemy defenses to destroy assigned targets. The basic nuclear effects about which more knowledge is needed are communications and radar blackout, argus effects, blast (especially high yield), shock-wave propagation, ground motion, radiation, electromagnetic pulse, and thermal. It seems quite possible that there are other high yield effects completely unknown to American technicians.

General Power, as Commander-in-Chief of the Strategic Air Command, testified from an operational point of view on the seriousness of the lack of effects knowledge. He said, "Now there are great voids in our knowledge on such things [deleted], shockwave propagation, blackout, communications and control that, in my opinion, can be obtained only

---

[37] *Preparedness Investigating Subcommittee Hearings, op. cit.,* p. 511.

by testing in the atmosphere."[38] He explained that he was responsible for the strategic war plans, and that he has to deal with known data. "If too much of the data is extrapolated or theoretical, I do not have a high confidence factor that I have a sound plan," he said.[39]

It was clear from the testimony before the two Senate committees that the United States certainly, and the Soviet Union probably, is not in possession of enough effects knowledge to resolve the doubts that exist about the design and survivability of nuclear weapons, hardened facilities, and communications. Most of the effects data that the United States has were learned from tests prior to the moratorium and are of only limited value, because these tests were only exploratory and not directed to the specific problems of today's weapons systems. Two subsequent test series were planned for 1959 but were canceled because of the moratorium.[40] Then in 1960 planning for nuclear effects tests was discontinued, and the 1962 test series was severely limited by both lack of preparation and the political restrictions described above. No information on high yield effects was obtained at all, and unfortunately this information cannot be extrapolated.[41] Further, since effects vary with yield, altitude, and time of day, a great number of tests are needed to compile a respectable body of data. According to the testimony of Col. Roy Clinton, it was agreed in the scientific community that the most important effects test to be done was a high yield surface test, but this could not be done on the short time scale imposed by political authority.[42]

Since the Test Ban Treaty would preclude further effects

---

[38] *Ibid.,* p. 721.

[39] *Ibid.,* p. 780.

[40] *Ibid.,* p. 160.

[41] U.S. Atomic Energy Commission, *News Release Nr. D-279,* October 31, 1961.

[42] *Preparedness Investigating Subcommittee Hearings, op. cit.,* p. 163.

testing, it is particularly important to know just how much the Soviet Union knows about nuclear effects, but intelligence sources could not learn to what degree their tests were instrumented and how successful their instrumentation was. Hence this information simply is not available. This fact renders the risk of failing to gain further knowledge of effects incalculable. The risk could be anything from negligible to disastrous.

As might be expected in such a case, the opinions of experts and officials vary widely as to the relative position of the United States and the Soviet Union. General Le May said that he was convinced that the Soviets "have gotten a lot more information on weapons effects than we have and they may have uncovered some weakness that they can exploit."[43] Col. Thorne believed that the complexity and operational nature of the Soviet systems indicate that they are ahead.[44] Dr. Teller stated that the Soviets had a "decisive lead" because they had exploded three or four times as much as the United States since 1958, and he assumed that they looked at the effects of these explosions as they apply to the ABM, penetration, and weapons vulnerability problems.[45] General Schriever testified: "I believe that they have definitely conducted considerably more effects tests than we have, and they should have more effects information than we have."[46]

On the other hand, Dr. Brown, Dr. Bradbury, and Dr. Seaborg do not believe that the Soviets know more than we do. Their position was that the Soviets may know some things that we do not, and the United States may know some things that they do not know. None would say that they believed the United States to be ahead, however. Obviously a firm esti-

---

43 *Ibid.*, p. 383.
44 *Ibid.*, p. 357.
45 *Foreign Relations Committee Hearings, op. cit.*, p. 482.
46 *Preparedness Investigating Subcommittee Hearings, op. cit.*, p. 385.

mate of which side is ahead in the effects field is impossible because of a dearth of hard intelligence; however, it is clear that the Soviet Union has had the opportunity to learn more than the United States, and therefore it would seem prudent to assume that they made the most of their opportunity. To assume otherwise would amount to coloring a vital estimate with wishful thinking. One can only conclude that there exists an urgent need for more information on the effects of nuclear explosions, which can be gained only through testing in the atmosphere.

Antiballistic Missiles (ABM)

The history of military technology has been a story of the struggle between the offense and the defense. At times the offense has been dominant, at other times the defense has been stronger; it has been a see-saw battle. In World War I the machine gun was a formidable defensive weapon until the British developed the tank. Then the offense once again became supreme. In the prelude to World War II the British development of radar to counter Nazi offensive air power played an important role in the resulting struggle. Today the ballistic missile is an offensive weapon so powerful that strategic nuclear war has become unprofitable, and since there has been no defense against catastrophic destruction there has been no nuclear war. But both the Soviet Union and the United States have devoted considerable effort to developing a defense against ballistic missiles.

This is perhaps the most difficult task science has ever undertaken. A missile warhead is a small object which travels through space at a speed of about fifteen thousand miles per hour, twenty times the speed of sound. Knocking down such a projectile is an extremely demanding task. It involves capacity to acquire the target early, to discriminate decoys from warheads, to handle large volumes of traffic, and to hit and kill the small, rapidly moving warhead. At present the system being developed by the United States for this task consists of several types of radar, two types of interceptor missiles, and a system of very complex computing equipment to control the radars and direct the interceptor missile. If the incoming warhead could be directly hit by a solid object it would be destroyed, but this appears to be technically impossible. The alternative, then, is to reduce the need for impossible pinpoint accuracy by adding a nuclear warhead to the defensive missile, which will have a considerable lethal radius. If the defensive warhead can be exploded in the proximity of the offensive warhead, the defensive mission will be accomplished.

If an effective defense against missiles can be developed, its importance is obvious. If either the U.S. or the U.S.S.R. were to develop an effective defense while the other did not, the loser would be at the mercy of the winner. Even if a partially effective system could be developed, it would serve to save millions of lives, many of the nation's cities, industries, and retaliatory capability. Considering that there are many unanswered questions about the survivability of United States hardened sites, a partially effective ABM could go a long ways toward enhancing the survivability of the retaliatory forces and thus increase the deterrent credibility. Another use for a partially effective ABM would be protection against proliferation. Even though the system may not be effective against the highly sophisticated Soviet offense, an ABM effective against anything that China or any other newcomer to the nuclear club might produce is not so difficult to accomplish and would serve as a deterrent to proliferation. A partially effective ABM system would be equally useful from the Soviet point of view. It could protect them against proliferation in the same manner that it would be useful to the United States. Further, although the vulnerability of the United States retaliatory forces may not be so great as to insure the Russians against a crippling United States counter blow, a partially effective ABM combined with some degree of vulnerability of the second-strike force to Soviet attack might provide the Soviet leadership with sufficient insurance to enable them to consider an attack profitable. From these considerations it is clear that a vigor- · ous ABM program is absolutely essential to national security. To fall behind the Soviet Union in defensive weapons would be courting disaster to an even greater degree than falling behind in the offensive competition.

In spite of the overriding importance of ballistic missile defense, it has been said that it is impossible. In fact President Kennedy, in his press conference of August 1, 1963, said: "The problem of developing a defense against a missile is beyond us and beyond the Soviets technically, and I think many who work on it feel that it can never be accomplished. . . ."[47] There were few officials and experts who testified at the test ban hearings who agreed, however. Dr. John Foster said of the President's statement, "I think that is an overstatement,"[48] and Dr. Teller said: "The recent high-powered public statement that it is beyond us is in itself, I think, something that may harmfully influence our efforts."[49] He went on to say: "There is little doubt in my mind that ballistic missile defense is possible if we spend enough money."[50] The testimony of Col. Le Van, General Wheeler's project officer on ballistic missile defense, directly conflicted with the President's statement. He said:

I personally interviewed a number of scientists and en-

---

[47] "Text of President Kennedy's August 1 Press Conference," *Congressional Quarterly Weekly Report*, August 9, 1963, p. 1415.
[48] *Preparedness Investigating Subcommittee Hearings, op. cit.*, p. 491.
[49] *Ibid.*, p. 575.
[50] *Ibid.*, p. 769.

gineers working in this area for the Army. We made quite an evaluation using our in-house staff.

In summation it turns out that one can design an effective antimissile missile system. . . .[51]

It would seem that on this vital subject, the President either had been poorly advised or did not express himself clearly. The fact is that the Soviet Union had at this time deployed antiballistic missiles around both Leningrad and Moscow,[52] and while the United States has not deployed its Nike Zeus, both General Taylor and General Wheeler had recommended that it be deployed. The Nike Zeus was sufficiently effective to intercept an Atlas missile, launched from Vandenburg, California, on Kwajalein Island in the Pacific, but it was not sufficiently effective, in the opinion of Secretary of Defense McNamara, to warrant deployment. A follow-on system, the Nike X, is now being developed; it includes the Zeus missile and employs improved radar, improved computers, and another missile, the Sprint, for low altitude interception. Whether or not this system will be deployed remains to be seen. Secretary McNamara has estimated that "to protect twenty-odd metropolitan centers, containing some 35 per cent of the population perhaps, would cost on the order of 14 billion."[53] But that the United States is really serious about missile defense is clearly evident in the fact that up to January 1, 1965, about $2.5 billion has been spent on this project.[54] With this much money being spent, it does not seem likely that missile defense "is beyond us," as President Kennedy said, even though a perfect and fool-proof defense may not be achieved in the near future.

There was no general agreement as to who is ahead in

---

[51] *Ibid.,* p. 671.

[52] *Ibid.,* p. 734.

[53] *Foreign Relations Committee Hearings, op. cit.,* p. 163.

[54] Michael Gether, "New A-ICBM City Defense," *Missiles and Rockets,* January 18, 1965, p. 3.

the quest for missile defense. While no one would say that the United States was ahead, Secretary McNamara and Dr. Brown said:

> The best present judgment is that our development efforts are comparable in magnitude and success with those of the Soviets. Any deployed system which the Soviets are likely to have now or in the near future does not appear to be as effective, certainly not more effective than Nike-Zeus.[55]

Dr. Teller took direct issue with this judgment and flatly stated that the Soviets are ahead because of their superior knowledge of weapons effects.[56] He told the Foreign Relations Committee: "What we must say is that they had three or perhaps four times more opportunity to find out the relevant facts on missile defense than we had,"[57] and that the Soviet ABM program is both older and stronger than that of the United States. As for the McNamara-Brown evaluation of the deployed Soviet ABM, he said:

> Their [the Soviet] system is different from the Nike-Zeus. We have naturally an opinion that what we have designed is best. Not knowing all details it is in my opinion impossible to make a statement of the kind which I had just read to you [the McNamara-Brown statement quoted above] with complete confidence.[58]

Dr. Foster, General Le May, and General Twining tended to agree with Dr. Teller, and the official JCS statement said: ". . . in the ABM field the Soviets may possess some information not available to the United States."[59] Admiral Anderson took a cautious stand and warned: "I don't think anyone of

---

[55] *Preparedness Investigating Subcommittee Hearings, op. cit.,* p. 860, and *Foreign Relations Committee Hearings, op. cit.,* pp. 103-104. The two officials used identical wording.

[56] *Foreign Relations Committee Hearings, op. cit.,* pp. 549–51.

[57] *Ibid.,* pp. 922–23.

[58] *Ibid.,* p. 768.

[59] *Ibid.,* p. 275.

us can say with absolute certainty the degree to which the Russians have progressed in developing an effective anti-ballistic missile defense."[60] It is interesting to note that, while it is well known that both Leningrad and Moscow are protected by antiballistic missiles, Secretary McNamara told the Foreign Relations Committee: "I do not believe that their [the Soviets] metropolitan centers are today protected by operational ballistic missile systems."[61] His statement was challenged by Senator Thurmond, who declared: "Secretary McNamara several days ago testified under oath that the Communists had no antiballistic missile system, when he had previously testified before the Armed Services Committee and supplied the details on the system [deleted]. So I call that to the attention of the chairman, which is a direct false statement."[62] On balance, the fact of the matter seemed to be that the Soviets have deployed an ABM while the United States has not, but did have the option of doing so. Because of a lack of hard intelligence it is probably impossible to say with any degree of confidence just what the comparative state of the art with respect to missile defense is, but almost certainly the United States is not ahead. This situation should be an imperative for hard, bold, and imaginative work rather than pessimism or skepticism.

Official Soviet spokesmen have manifested neither skepticism nor pessimism concerning missile defense, but claim that they have solved the problem. Since Khrushchev's often-quoted statement in July, 1962, that the Soviet Union has an antimissile missile that "can hit a fly in outer space,"[63] public Soviet claims have multiplied rapidly. They became particularly pronounced following the display of the November 7, 1963, military parade in Red Square of a new type of sur-

---

60 *Preparedness Investigating Subcommittee Hearings, op. cit.,* p. 313.
61 *Foreign Relations Committee Hearings, op. cit.,* p. 114.
62 *Preparedness Investigating Subcommittee Hearings, op. cit.,* p. 734.
63 *New York Times,* July 17, 1962.

face-to-air missile, which Soviet commentary placed in the antimissile class.[64] Marshal Biriuzov, Chief of the General Staff, asserted on November 8, for example, that the Soviet armed forces now possessed antimissile weapons "capable of intercepting any missile in the air. This circumstance," he said, "permits our country to be defended against any attack."[65] A similar emphatic claim was made a few days later by a Soviet artillery general, who said: "These long-range, air defense missiles are capable of destroying any means of air-space attack."[66] Air Force Marshal V. Sudets, Commander of the National PVO and the man immediately responsible for any actual operations against a missile attack, was just a shade less categorical in January, 1964, when he stated:

> The combat capabilities of the weapons of these [PVO] forces permit the destruction of practically all modern means of air-space attack, at maximum range, high and low altitudes, and supersonic speeds.[67]

With the United States at best about equal with the Soviet Union, and possibly behind, the important question is, will the Test Ban Treaty adversely affect American progress? Many critical problems of ABM development, such as reaction speed, missile performance, traffic handling capacity, decoy discrimination, and radar development, depend upon non-nuclear information, but there are three areas that are also critical and do depend upon nuclear knowledge. These are: (1) the effects of nuclear explosions upon radar, especially blackout; (2) warhead development; and (3) lethality of the warhead. Each of these problems was explored in the hearings.

---

[64] *Ibid.*, November 8, 1963.

[65] *Izvestia,* November 8, 1963.

[66] Major General I. Baryshev, "Nuclear Weapons and P.V.O.," *Red Star,* November 12, 1963, p. 4.

[67] *Izvestia,* January 5, 1964.

Blackout is a severe problem in missile defense because both offensive and defensive nuclear explosions will blind the system, rendering it ineffective for a period of time. Obviously the more that is known about the blackout problem the better it can be circumvented. Expert testimony revealed that it would be highly desirable to learn more about blackout through atmospheric testing, but that with present knowledge the problem could be accommodated. One way around the problem would be to deploy more radars so that the scene of action can be viewed from various locations and angles. The difficulty with this solution is that it is very costly, and the ultimate decision to deploy the system will depend upon Secretary McNamara's cost-effectiveness analysis. If the system becomes too costly, it may not be deployed. An alternative solution would be to develop a new type of ABM warhead, designed to reduce blackout. This type of warhead could be developed by underground testing, but only through atmospheric testing could the warhead be evaluated.[68] Under the Test Ban Treaty this cannot be accomplished. One must conclude, then, that the Test Ban Treaty presents an expensive but not insurmountable obstacle in this problem area.

There is no doubt that a suitable warhead for the Nike-X can be developed through underground testing; but without atmospheric testing an optimum warhead cannot be produced.[69] The difference that the Test Ban Treaty makes, then, is the difference between a "satisfactory" warhead and an "optimum" warhead. This, of course, degrades the effectiveness of the system.

The problem of lethality involves knowing the lethal radius of the warhead at a particular altitude. Near the sur-

---

[68] *Foreign Relations Committee Hearings, op. cit.,* p. 615.

[69] *Ibid.,* p. 159. See also *Preparedness Investigating Subcommittee Hearings, op. cit.,* p. 439.

face of the earth, blast and shock are the two main kill mechanisms; however, higher in the atmosphere, they become less effective and radiation becomes more important. Above the atmosphere, radiation is the only effective kill mechanism. The problem is that data from high altitude tests and theories are incomplete with respect to these radiations, and the same is true of the blast and shock data at lower altitudes. Under the Test Ban Treaty this information cannot be obtained, so there will be some doubt as to just what the lethal radius of any given warhead is. The way around this problem is to overdesign, but as in the case of blackout and radars, this process will raise the cost of the system.

In sum, it is possible that an antiballistic missile can be developed without atmospheric testing, but it will be more costly and less effective than with atmospheric testing and, perhaps most important, its exact effectiveness will not be known. When it comes to the decision to deploy this weapon and Secretary McNamara puts its cost versus its effectiveness through his cost-effectiveness decision-making process, the difference between a system developed with atmospheric testing and one developed under the Test Ban Treaty may deny the United States the benefits of ballistic missile defense. In the field of ballistic missile defense, then, the Test Ban Treaty will at least cost the American people considerable money and protection and at worst it will deny them any defense at all. This is of the utmost importance because, if the Soviet Union produces an effective missile defense while the United States either does not or fails to deploy a system because it is too expensive, the credibility of the American deterrent will have vanished. As Joseph Alsop recently said:

> Strategically, politically, and in every other imaginable way, the United States will gain from possessing a defensive system of this kind. In such a situation as Britain faced in 1939, there is all the difference in the world between a price tag on surrender amounting to the end of civilized life in the United

States, and a price tag that may be very terrible yet still preserves the future for later generations of free Americans.[70]

Penetration

Ballistic missile defense and warhead penetration of defenses are opposite sides of the same coin. If the enemy has no ballistic missile defense, then there is no need to worry about penetration. But since the Soviet Union already has an operational ABM and has an extensive research and development program at least as advanced as that of the United States, the penetration problem must be considered. Penetration can be accomplished by saturation, disruption or destruction of the enemy defenses, by hardening warheads to blast and radiation, or by a combination of these means. Current U.S. penetration philosophy concentrates on saturation and is dominated by decoy design and salvo techniques, although there has been considerable work done on the hardening of warheads to nuclear explosion effects. This work has been restricted by the limited knowledge of weapons effects. The importance of this program was brought out by Commissioner Haworth. He said: "The AEC attaches particular importance to the continuation of a program to determine and reduce the vulnerability of nuclear warheads in defensive environments."[71] This program would definitely be inhibited by the Test Ban Treaty because improvements in hardening are dependent upon knowledge of atmospheric effects, although some progress could be made with underground tests combined with extrapolations and theory.[72] Dr. John Foster explained this problem as follows:

[70] *Washington Post,* January 13, 1965.
[71] *Preparedness Investigating Subcommittee Hearings, op. cit.,* p. 248.
[72] *See* the testimony of Dr. Leland J. Haworth, *Preparedness Investigating Subcommittee Hearings, op. cit.,* pp. 251–52.

Suppose that the USSR were to develop a defense such that our ability to penetrate might depend upon a saturation attack. For this application specially designed hardened warheads might be required.

Considerable progress on such warheads can be made with underground tests, but under the treaty again, the crucial atmospheric experiments to determine if the warhead actually has the necessary hardness against combined radiation and shock effects would be prohibited. We might thereby be denied assurance of such a penetration capability.[73]

General Le May expressed the problem from a military point of view:

We must know at what distance currently programmed missile reentry vehicles, such as those for Minuteman and Polaris, would be destroyed by a defensive explosion. We need this information as a function of altitude and yield as well as other characteristics of defensive weapons so that steps may be taken to reduce vulnerability and to improve aids and tactics for penetration.

We need effects data so that follow-on reentry systems can be designed to be as invulnerable as possible to interception and destruction. . . . Only after nuclear tests [in the atmosphere] can we confidently proceed to develop hardening of our reentry vehicles and warheads.[74]

It was brought out in the hearings that an atmospheric test series to determine the information pertinent to penetration had been planned, but of course cannot be accomplished under the Test Ban Treaty.

Secretary McNamara, however, did not share the concern expressed by General Le May, Commissioner Haworth, Dr. Foster, and others. He told the Foreign Relations Committee:

---

[73] *Foreign Relations Committee Hearings, op. cit.,* p. 615.
[74] *Preparedness Investigating Subcommittee Hearings, op. cit.,* pp. 353–54.

But, regardless of the design of any Soviet ABM system . . . the United States will continue to have the capability, and most importantly the Soviets will know that we will continue to have the capability—to penetrate and to devastate the Soviet Union if a retaliatory blow is required.[75]

The Secretary's words are indeed comforting, but they are in sharp contrast to those of the scientist responsible for developing the warhead, Dr. Foster, and the General responsible for the war plans and, if need be, for their implementation, General Le May. The Secretary was relying on a saturation attack by a large number of missiles, which is at best a risky business, especially when none of the missiles have been completely tested from launch to explosion and the vulnerability of the hardened launch complexes to nuclear attack has never been tested and is, in fact, based upon very incomplete knowledge of nuclear effects. The very fact that a test series to determine warhead vulnerability and improve penetration was planned shows that this information is needed, and the testimony of Commissioner Haworth, Dr. Foster, and General Le May adds emphasis to the fact.

---

[75] *Foreign Relations Committee Hearings, op. cit.,* pp. 104–5.

chapter 4

CLANDESTINE TESTING AND ITS DETECTION

The negotiations concerning a test ban treaty, which had been conducted almost continuously since 1958, had presumedly failed for just one reason: the United States insisted on an inspection system to preclude clandestine testing by the Soviet Union, while the Soviet Union refused to agree to any reasonable inspection system. The main problem area, however, was the detection of clandestine underground tests; the great merit of the limited test ban treaty was supposed to be that, since underground testing is permitted, the risk of clandestine testing would be eliminated. The Senate hearings proved this argument to be less than completely valid.

From the Soviets' record in international relations there is no question that Communists will cheat and deceive in any way they can to further their goals. The breach of the moratorium and the Cuban crisis of 1962 are two recent reminders of this well-known fact. American officials recognize this, but they still minimize the risk of Soviet violations. For example, President Kennedy told the American people in his television speech to the nation on July 26, 1963:

A ban on nuclear tests . . . requires inspection only for underground tests. This nation now possesses a variety of techniques to detect the nuclear tests of other nations which are conducted in the air or under water.

. . . .

The treaty initiated yesterday . . . prohibits only those tests that we ourselves can police.

It is also true, as Mr. Khrushchev would agree, that nations cannot afford in these matters simply to rely on the good faith of their adversaries. We have therefore not overlooked the risk of secret violations. There is at present a possibility that deep in outerspace, that hundreds of thousands and millions of miles away from the earth illegal tests might go undetected. But we already have the capability to construct a system of observation that would make such tests impossible to conceal.[1]

And in his message to the Senate accompanying the treaty the President said:

The risks in clandestine violations under this treaty are far smaller than the risks in unlimited testing. Underground tests will still be available for weapons development; and other tests, to be significant, must run substantial risks of detection. No nation tempted to violate the treaty can be certain that an attempted violation will go undetected, given the many means of detecting nuclear explosions. The risk of detection outweigh the potential gains from violation.[2]

Both of these statements, rather than expressing a black and white fact, express official judgment on a highly complex and controversial matter. As the President implied, the United States had no capability of detecting tests in space, and certainly could not detect and identify *all* tests in the atmosphere and underwater. Secretary McNamara readily admitted: "I don't believe that we can say that the present capability will give assurance of detecting all such explosions."[3] The Joint Chiefs of Staff, worried about the possibility of clandestine testing, insisted that the American detection system be improved.[4] Clearly there is a risk of clandestine testing, and how great that risk might be is a very difficult and complex question that must be explored. The

---

[1] John F. Kennedy, "The Nuclear Test Ban Treaty: A Step Towards Peace (An Address to the Nation on July 26, 1963)," *Department of State Bulletin,* August 12, 1963, p. 234.

[2] "President Kennedy's Treaty Message to the Senate," *Congressional Quarterly Weekly Report,* August 16, 1963, p. 1457.

[3] *Foreign Relations Committee Hearings, op. cit.,* p. 141.

[4] *Ibid.,* p. 318.

political leadership of the nation said that the risk was negligible, but other knowledgeable persons, such as Admiral Anderson,[5] General Le May,[6] Dr. Teller,[7] Admiral Burke,[8] and Admiral Strauss,[9] were seriously worried.

Assessment of the risk requires not only an examination of United States detection capability but also an estimate of what kinds of clandestine testing are possible and of what value they might be to the Soviet Union. The following discussion of these matters will be analyzed under three headings: atmospheric, space, and underwater testing.

Atmospheric Testing

There is considerable question about just how large an atmospheric explosion can escape detection, and this is influenced to some degree by how clean the explosion is. The cleaner the explosion, the more difficult it is to detect and identify because of the reduced fallout. But it is generally agreed that atmospheric tests under a kiloton cannot be effectively policed under any circumstances.[10] At an altitude of from six to twenty miles, an important altitude for conducting effects tests in connection with ABM systems, it is particularly difficult to detect and identify tests. Dr. Brown testified that at these difficult altitudes "identification should often be possible for yields of a few kilotons or more."[11] Unfortunately, this ambiguous statement was not clarified, and the question of "how often" and "how many kilotons" re-

---

[5] *Preparedness Investigating Subcommittee Hearings, op. cit.,* p. 334.
[6] *Ibid.,* p. 633.
[7] *Ibid.,* p. 563.
[8] *Ibid.,* p. 939.
[9] *Foreign Relations Committee Hearings, op. cit.,* p. 673.
[10] *Preparedness Investigating Subcommittee Hearings, op. cit.,* p. 334.
[11] *Ibid.,* p. 864.

mains. Tests near or on the surface of the earth would be easier to detect and Dr. Brown estimated that tests in the kiloton range are "likely to be detected."[12] He said that detection in the atmosphere could be improved by installation of a satellite surveillance system, which the United States did not currently have, but that this would be very expensive. Dr. Teller doubted the effectiveness of a satellite system, saying, "I believe that in trying to rely on such methods, which raise our suspicions [that a test has been conducted], but which may not give us proof of violation, we are really building castles of sand."[13]

Clearly there is a level of yield, at least a kiloton on or near the surface and more in the upper atmosphere, where detection and identification are impossible or unlikely, and a somewhat higher yield at which a violation can be detected but not identified. Whether the Soviets would be cautious or bold in their violations is an open question, and an equally open question is how vigorously the United States would protest a series of suspected, but not clearly proven, violations. The record of the past would indicate that the Soviet Union would be bold, while the United States would be cautious. If this proved to be the case, it would have the effect of raising the threshold of detection and would give the Soviet Union an added margin of safety for clandestine low yield tests.

In the upper atmosphere the principal purpose of clandestine tests would be to learn more about weapons effects. Dr. Brown felt that the tests that could escape detection would be too small to be of significant value,[14] but he did admit that undetectable tests could lead to a better understanding of radar blackout, and, to a limited degree, of determining ABM warhead vulnerability. Contrary to Dr.

---

12 *Ibid.*
13 *Ibid.*, p. 546.
14 *Foreign Relations Committee Hearings, op. cit.,* p. 186.

Brown, Dr. Teller felt that these tests could be significant[15] for ballistic missile defense.

Dr. Teller expressed particular concern about tests conducted near, on, and just under the surface of the earth for the purpose of determining vulnerability of United States hardened missile sites. He explained to the Preparedness Investigating Subcommittee:

> According to the letter of the treaty, it is possible to bury a nuclear explosive a foot or a fraction of a foot underground. As a result, the relevant shock effects can be reasonably reproduced, they can be put into the air; and, in addition, a considerable, though perhaps not sufficient, amount can be learned concerning [deleted] effects. According to the letter of the treaty, such an explosion is an underground explosion. We can make the explosion clean enough so that no fission activity will be detected outside the United States. Thus, the treaty will permit the execution of the experiment.

> On the other hand, experiments carried out deep underground are not sufficient to obtain the relevant information. Shocks generated by such underground explosions have a different nature from those which one obtains from aerial bursts or shallow buried bursts. Any attempt for exploring the [deleted] underground runs into great difficulty due to the disturbing effect of the surrounding earth on the walls of the cavity in which the experiment may be carried out.

> The situation is rendered particularly dangerous because the Russians can explore effects upon our Minuteman sites by small clandestine experiments in the atmosphere and by bigger shallowly buried literally legal underground experiments. These two types of experiments complement each other, the former, that is experiments in the air, giving needed variability as to the effects of the surrounding, while the latter can determine the dependence of observed effects on the size of the explosions within wide ranges. A shallow underground experiment will be noticed, but is legal.

---

15 *Preparedness Investigating Subcommittee Hearings, op. cit.,* p. 770.

If the Russians should discover by such experimentation that our missile sites are vulnerable to a certain type of attack while we are ignorant of the relevant facts, our main retaliatory force could be neutralized. Atlas and Titan sites are generally more vulnerable than Minuteman sites. Our Polaris missiles are fewer in number; while they remain safe as long as their location is not detected their continued safety depends on our ability to keep ahead of Russian anti-submarine measures.

The above discussion shows that Russian violation of the treaty in the subkiloton range may endanger U. S. security. It further shows that this danger will be greatly aggravated if we fail to carry out shallow underground experiments which are permitted by the wording of the treaty. In case the treaty should be ratified, it is of great importance to make certain that shallow underground explosions will indeed be carried out by our side in such a manner as to obtain maximum information from these experiments.[16]

Dr. Harold Brown did not share Dr. Teller's concern, but in his consideration of the problem he did not take into account the possibility of the Soviet Union's exploding a very clean large yield device slightly under the surface of the earth. If the fallout were so slight that it did not go beyond the borders of the Soviet Union, it would not be a violation of the treaty. If a little fallout did drift beyond the Soviet borders and was picked up by the United States detection system what would the United States do? What could it do?[17] No administration witness took this consideration

16 *Ibid.*, p. 549.

17 On January 15, 1965, the Soviet Union violated the treaty by conducting a presumed underground test that released radioactive material into the atmosphere. This radioactive debris was detected by the American detection system, proving that the radioactivity had passed well beyond Soviet borders. The Atomic Energy Commission announced on January 16 that the Soviet Union had conducted the biggest underground test in its history, and tentatively estimated its force at one hundred kilotons. On January 19, the Atomic Energy Commission upgraded the blast to the intermediate range (two hundred kilotons to one megaton). The Seis-

into account. Dr. Brown argued that illegal surface bursts

might be attempted in order to obtain information on the effects of nuclear explosion on hardened missile sites and for static tests of reentry vehicles. A good deal of this information can be obtained from underground tests; however, to study the coupling into the ground and [deleted] effects, require very large bursts at or above the surface. To gain this information very elaborate equipment and construction would be necessary. As an example, U.S. experiments of this kind have taken up to 6 months or a year to prepare, and the same thing seems to be true for Soviet tests. Finally, it should be pointed out that suggested U.S. test proposals have always emphasized the difficulties of scaling in yield; the tests of a few kilotons which have been carried out appear unsatisfactory for reducing the uncertainties in ranges of effects below a factor of [deleted]. High-yield tests [deleted] have always been considered an appropriate next step in this connection, and preliminary U.S. planning has gone forward for such tests. And even a few kilotons is detectable, so that these are not undetectable tests on any basis.[18]

In summary, it seems clear that the Soviet Union can do some clandestine testing in the atmosphere and on the sur-

---

mological Institution at Uppsala University in Sweden estimated the force at a megaton, and a Swedish scientific expert said that the signals received indicated that it was the first underground explosion of a hydrogen bomb.

The U.S. State Department's first reaction was to ask the Soviet Ambassador for an explanation of the event. On January 25 the Soviet Ambassador denied that the Soviet Union had violated the treaty. He admitted that radioactive debris had vented into the atmosphere, but claimed that the quantity was so insignificant as to preclude the possibilities of a violation of the treaty. The next day William C. Foster, Director of the United States Arms Control and Disarmament Agency, told the House Foreign Affairs Committee that he was convinced that the venting was accidental and that the Test Ban Treaty had not been violated. Finally, on March 9, the State Department issued an official statement to the effect that the Soviet test "may have constituted a technical violation," but did not represent a threat to national security.

[18] *Preparedness Investigating Subcommittee Hearings, op. cit.,* p. 867.

face that may be of value to them in developing an ABM system and in searching for vulnerabilities in United States hardened retaliatory systems. The degree of risk is impossible for the layman to judge accurately since the best scientists disagree. In this uncomfortable situation the only thing that will help resolve the doubt is an improved detection capability supplemented by a vastly improved conventional intelligence system to provide better knowledge of Soviet capabilities and activities. It is, of course, possible that there is no danger of clandestine atmospheric tests because the Soviets already know what they need to know, but this again is another area of question and doubt because intelligence cannot provide the answers.

Testing in Space

The United States has very little capability for detecting nuclear tests in deep space, but a highly classified earth satellite system is under development. It should be noted that no decision has been made to deploy this system; it is simply under development. Dr. Harold Brown said that if and when this system is deployed, it could detect an unshielded test of ten kilotons at one hundred million kilometers, but that shielded tests of several megatons could escape detection at thirty million kilometers.[19] Dr. Teller disagreed. He said that up to five hundred kilotons unshielded can escape detection even if five hundred million dollars per year were spent on such a system.[20]

It was agreed among the scientists that nuclear tests in space are feasible, although they would be very costly and very difficult to accomplish. The purpose of such testing

---

[19] *Ibid.*, p. 869.
[20] *Ibid.*, pp. 546–47, 560.

would probably be limited to weapons development, determination of effects, and tests aimed at midcourse intercept of ballistic missiles. As for weapons development tests, since yields of up to a megaton can be exploded underground, only much higher yields would seem to be of interest to a violator. They would be very difficult and expensive to carry out since they would involve heavy payloads and separate instrument pods. Dr. Brown estimated that such tests would cost from fifty million to one hundred million dollars per shot, take several months to reach the test location, and involve serious reliability problems.[21] He concluded: "A program of a number of such tests would not be impossibly expensive for the Soviets, but could only be justified on the basis of benefits which we do not foresee. . . ." Dr. Seaborg's testimony on this point agreed with that of Dr. Brown.

As for exploring the possibility of developing a midcourse intercept system, Dr. Brown said:

> Effects test of this type are extremely expensive and only justifiable if potential savings run into hundreds of millions of dollars. Such tests appear not to be worth the effort involved in the near future and may never become attractive.[22]

Concerning this line of reasoning, Dr. Teller said, "I have learned by sad experience that in these important matters our imagination is limited."[23] It is indeed a basic axiom of the craft of intelligence that plans must be based on enemy capabilities rather than enemy intentions, and this requires knowledge applied to imagination. Violation of this axiom often results in unpleasant surprises. Recent history has shown that the Soviets have a great capacity for surprising the American political leadership; Sputnik, the breach of the moratorium, and the 1962 Cuban crisis are three significant

---

[21] *Ibid.*, p. 866.
[22] *Ibid.*
[23] *Ibid.*, p. 770.

recent examples. If American imagination is limited, the Soviet Union may again surprise the political leadership with an act, perhaps testing in space, which they thought to be "not worth the effort involved." Yet Secretary McNamara told the Foreign Relations Committee: "I conclude that as a practical matter, illegal clandestine testing in deep space is not a reasonable proposition for the Soviet Union."[24] Dr. Teller replied: "I believe this reflects the Secretary's great reliance on intelligence. I hope that he is right, I fear that he may not be."[25]

Underwater Testing

Detecting nuclear explosions under the high seas may not be a difficult task and the coordination of existing sensors with the Atomic Energy Detection System should suffice to do the job. Underwater explosions of only a few pounds can often be detected with hydrophones from great distances. Further, testing under the high seas would require considerable ship movements and concentrations that are extremely vulnerable to normal intelligence collecting activity. Underwater testing in internal lakes, such as Lake Baikal, can be detected by seismic means, but relatively small tests could go unidentified. Testing in inland waters, however, holds the overriding disadvantage of contaminating the water and the plant and animal life that lives in it and is therefore generally considered to be unprofitable.

It would seem that there is less motivation for conducting clandestine tests underwater than in the atmosphere, because many underwater effects measurements can be obtained from high explosive charges. There would be some motiva-

---

[24] *Foreign Relations Committee Hearings, op. cit.,* p. 448.
[25] *Ibid.*

tion for conducting nuclear tests to determine effects on submarines; however, there is no doubt that if a nuclear device is exploded in the vicinity of a submarine, the submarine will be destroyed, and knowledge of the exact distance at which a given yield will destroy a submarine is of no great importance. The primary problems of antisubmarine warfare are detection, location, and identification. Given these factors, kill is certain enough.

Summary

In summary, then, the primary immediate risks of clandestine testing are a series of small atmospheric explosions and larger surface explosions for the purpose of gaining knowledge concerning ABM systems and hardened site vulnerability. In the future, with the development of further knowledge of space, tests in deep space may become a risk, especially if the United States fails to deploy an earth satellite system to detect such tests and fails to improve its conventional intelligence.

It is clear that clandestine tests are a risk, but just how serious a risk is difficult to judge. Certainly it is serious enough to warrant an expansion of the Atomic Energy Detection System as well as serious improvement of conventional intelligence. If intelligence fails to detect Soviet preparations and seriously misjudges Soviet activity and preparations, as it did from 1958 to 1961 when they were preparing for the huge 1961 test series, then the risk of clandestine testing is very serious. So the risk depends to a large degree on what the United States does to reduce the risk through improved intelligence and detection. Perhaps the best summary judgment expressed to the Senate was that of the Joint Chiefs of Staff in their formal statement:

Such disadvantages as might accrue to the United States under conditions of honest fulfillment of the treaty conditions would be further aggravated if the Soviets successfully tested by illicit explosions in the atmosphere, underwater, or in outer space. By such clandestine testing, they might carry out investigations of weapons effects in the field of ballistic missiles, ballistic missile defense, antisubmarine warfare, and high yield technology, the latter only if the testing were done in outer space. However, the dangers of detection and the cost and difficulty of testing in outer space would tend to impose severe restrictions upon such clandestine testing. Other clandestine tests in the atmosphere or underwater, depending upon their size, would involve a fairly high probability of detection by our conventional intelligence and our atomic energy detection system. Moreover, the Joint Chiefs of Staff consider the resulting progress which the Soviets might make clandestinely to be a relatively minor factor in relation to the overall present and probable balance of military strength *if adequate safeguards are maintained.*[26]

What the Joint Chiefs seemed to be telling the political leadership and the Senate is that they will go along with the risks of clandestine testing if, and only if, the Administration and the Senate will promise to execute the safeguards they recommend.

---

[26] *Ibid.*, p. 274; emphasis supplied. See also *Preparedness Investigating Subcommittee Hearings, op. cit.,* p. 589.

chapter 5

SOME STRATEGIC PROBLEMS

Nuclear testing in the atmosphere bears very heavily on several strategic problems faced by American defense planners. Some of the more important of these problems are (1) missile launch complex survivability, (2) missile reliability, (3) yield verification of stockpiled weapons, and (4) troop training. In order to evaluate the effect of the Test Ban Treaty upon United States defenses, each of these problems must be examined.

Survivability of Hardened Missile Launch Complexes

The two Senate committees took a large volume of testimony on the survivability of the missile launch complexes; however, the Preparedness Investigating Committee went into the matter in much greater detail than the Foreign Relations Committee. It also heard testimony from important military witnesses who did not appear before the Foreign Relations Committee, such as General Schriever, who was responsible for the design of the sites, and General Thomas S. Power, who was responsible for the war plans and commanded the systems. The basic question is: How certain is it that the missile force can absorb a Soviet first strike and be capable of dealing a devastating blow to the enemy? At stake is nothing less than the deterrent credibility and capability of the United States. Unfortunately there is no black and white answer to this vital question because of a lack of knowledge of high yield weapons effects and uncertainties in the design criteria of the launch complexes. In order to evaluate the problem properly, it is helpful to go into the background of the construction of the hardened sites.

The Titan I, the Atlas E and F, the Titan II, and the Minuteman are all hardened systems. General Schriever initiated the hardening program in 1957 when he ordered certain studies of the problem to be made. Since there was little effects data to go on, a technical advisory panel, composed of the best scientists in the country, was set up to advise on the hardness criteria. They did not have adequate confirmed information to work with, so atmospheric tests to determine needed data were planned for 1959 and 1960. These tests were never carried out because of the moratorium.[1] In the absence of sound experimental data they employed theoretical and extrapolated information, and then overdesigned to compensate for their lack of knowledge.

After the Soviet Union broke the moratorium in 1961 and the United States began planning for a new atmospheric test series, the need for effects data was urgent, and it was recognized that the most useful test to meet these needs would be a high yield surface burst near a silo. However, this is a very difficult test to accomplish and there was not enough time to prepare it in the time frame allowed for the series.[2] The data necessary to confirm the design criteria of the sites and urgently needed data on effects such as shock, ground motion, shock wave propagation, electromagnetic pulse, and the like could be gained through high yield atmospheric tests, but to date this has not been done. Low yield atmospheric and underground tests, which helped clarify uncertainties but did not remove them, were conducted. Col. Clinton testified:

---

[1] *Preparedness Investigating Subcommittee Hearings, op. cit.,* pp. 159–67.
[2] *Ibid.,* p. 163.

We have . . . gone to lower yields in which we have learned a great deal of information, and it has helped in proving out some of our theories, but it is not yet adequate to say that we know all the answers for a large yield surface burst.[3]

Dr. Harold Brown explained the situation this way:

The weapons effects relevant in this case of hardened sites . . . are thermal and pressure effects and ground motion effects [deleted]. There are substantial uncertainties in these areas. Our systems are designed, within the limits of our knowledge, so as to be on the safe side of the probabilities regarding these uncertainties.

By continued atmospheric testing, the United States could reduce present uncertainties in thermal and pressure effects and in hardness levels appropriate for the Minuteman silo. Uncertainties in ground motion effects and yield scaling [deleted] could also be reduced comparably.[4]

In the absence of enough hard knowledge to be sure of the design of the missile silos and the launch control facilities, General Schriever's group attempted to overdesign. All military and technical witnesses expressed high confidence that the design is adequate, but in the absence of detailed knowledge of nuclear effects, they could not be absolutely sure. That is one problem. Another problem is that a launch complex has never been tested against a high yield surface burst and therefore no one can be sure that the structure will function as designed. General Schriever told the Preparedness Investigating Subcommittee:

Now as the individual responsible for the development of these missiles, I can only say that there has to be a degree of uncertainty, and I could not put a percentage on that, in the absence of atmospheric testing.[5]

---

[3] *Ibid.*, p. 196.
[4] *Ibid.*, p. 864.
[5] *Ibid.*, p. 820.

The fact that General Schriever cannot put a percentage on the uncertainty is a very important point. If an exact degree of reliability or uncertainty of survival under given conditions can be established, then it can be taken into consideration in the war planning and a sound plan developed. But if the degree of uncertainty is unknown, then the workability of the war plan is unknown. As General Power said: "I have to have proven data, and if too much of the data is extrapolated or theoretical, I do not have a high confidence factor that I have a sound plan."[6]

All witnesses without exception agreed that there was a need to test the hardened missile launch complexes to verify their survivability and also to learn more about the effects they were designed to withstand. This can be done only by atmospheric testing. They also all agreed that there was a degree of uncertainty about both points, but where the disagreement lies is in the question of how serious a problem this is. Secretary McNamara felt sure of the survivability of the system. He said:

> The U.S. strategic missile force is designed to survive, and it will survive.
>
> Our missile force is deployed so as to assure that under any conceivable Soviet first strike, a substantial portion of it would remain in firing condition. Most of the land-based portion of the force has been hardened, as well as dispersed. Minuteman silos are designed to withstand thermal and pressure effects and ground motion effects of typical Soviet weapons detonated at relatively close quarters.
>
> The Minuteman control posts are protected by extreme hardening. In addition, we have duplicative facilities which will in the future include the capability of launching each individual Minuteman by a signal from airborne control posts.
>
> Large yield nuclear tests in the atmosphere, on or near the

---

6 *Ibid.,* p. 780.

ground, would help us to determine with greater precision the degree of hardness of our Minuteman silos.[7]

Taking issue with Secretary McNamara, Dr. Teller said that he was not sure whether the missile force would survive at present and even less sure that it would survive in the future.[8] He also argued that Secretary McNamara, in designing around the problem, was substituting brawn for brains. Building more and bigger launch complexes to compensate for a lack of knowledge that could be gained by testing was not only more expensive, he said, but also a step toward an arms race because it required building more weapons than would otherwise be necessary.[9]

General Power, General Le May, General Schriever, General Booth, and their staff assistants all urged continued testing to resolve uncertainties. General Taylor's position was in between that of Secretary McNamara and that of the Air Force generals. He said: "We have considered this restriction as one of the disabilities of the treaty, and consider it acceptable."[10] Just what an "acceptable disability" might be is not clear, nor is it clear why the United States should accept a disability when not necessary.

On balance, it appears that there is a problem in missile launch complex survivability, and one that is vital to the very survival of the nation. It would also seem that it may be taking an unwarranted risk for political authority to cast aside the judgment of the professional men who designed the system, operate it, and make the war plans. The Secretary of Defense may say there is no doubt, but when his opinion disagrees with his professional subordinates, who are his major sources of information and advice, the result is at least

---

[7] *Foreign Relations Committee Hearings, op. cit.,* p. 102.

[8] *Preparedness Investigating Subcommittee Hearings, op. cit.,* pp. 767–68.

[9] *Foreign Relations Committee Hearings, op. cit.,* p. 491.

[10] *Preparedness Investigating Subcommittee Hearings, op. cit.,* p. 620.

a little uncomfortable. Admiral Anderson summed up the matter modestly in these words:

> We are spending a lot of money . . . in building silos for our Minutemen, for our other weapons. It would be good to know whether they are sturdy enough or whether we could perhaps do with less bulk and strength in these.[11]

Missile Reliability

The nuclear test ban hearings revealed a great concern, and even alarm, in the military and scientific community about the reliability of the strategic missile system. The concern arose over the fact that of all the strategic missile systems in the American arsenal, only the Polaris has been tested from launch through detonation, and it has been tested only once. Secretary McNamara's position is that full scale tests are not necessary since the missile and the warhead have been tested separately. He maintains that there is no doubt that the combined components will work, but the military community and many scientists want to make sure. Prior to Secretary McNamara's term of office all military weapons, even the simple bayonet, were subject to exhaustive tests in their operational environment, but now the most complicated and delicate weapons ever produced have not been completely tested. On this point, the Joint Chiefs of Staff were unanimous in protesting the "no test" policy of the Secretary of Defense, but to no avail. General Le May had requested that such full scale tests be conducted during the 1962 test series, but the proposal was disapproved. Dr. Teller said of Mr. McNamara's policy:

> . . . the Secretary has also underestimated the importance of actual operational tests.

[11] *Ibid.*, p. 330.

He is willing to look at components. He doesn't care apparently whether all his components are put together and the working of the whole thing is investigated. It is like testing each part of the car but then not to give it a road test before you give it to the customer.[12]

Dr. John Foster explained the need for complete tests to the Foreign Relations Committee as follows:

Missile systems for offense or defense are extremely complex, yet must function not only under the ideal laboratory conditions in which they are usually tested, but also under the most adverse conditions—those of nuclear war.

I know of simpler systems which have not performed as expected—or which have actually failed—when proof-tested in environments which are far better understood than that of a hostile nuclear situation.

Technical people have had this experience not once but many times. That the exact nuclear environment for missiles, missile sites and reentry vehicles probably cannot be completely duplicated even without treaty restrictions is not an argument for no atmospheric tests whatever. We can obtain a much better understanding of the situation with nuclear experiments in the atmosphere than without them.[13]

General Power, Commander-in-Chief of the Strategic Air Command, which operates the strategic missiles, said that he had repeatedly requested full scale tests. When Mr. Russell Fee, special consultant for the Preparedness Investigating Subcommittee, reminded the General that he had been living with the absence of systems testing for a number of years, and asked why he couldn't continue to live with it, General Power snapped:

I didn't say you couldn't live with it. If you don't have it you will have to live with it. But if you ask me, should I live with it? Does it make sense to live with it? I would say no.[14]

---

[12] *Foreign Relations Committee Hearings, op. cit.,* p. 440.
[13] *Ibid.,* p. 615.
[14] *Preparedness Investigating Subcommittee Hearings, op. cit.,* p. 812.

General Power explained his need for full scale testing as follows:

> I have some [deleted] different types of nuclear weapons in the Strategic Air Command arsenal. None of them have been tested operationally from stockpile to detonation. I think this is a mistake. I think they should be tested.
>
> The way you can prove a weapon system is to take it out of the stockpile in a random pattern and let the tactical unit take it out and detonate it. If you haven't done this, there is always a chance that something has happened that we won't discover until too late. [Deleted.]
>
> The point I am making is that, unless you test the very thing that is in your arsenal, you are never certain, and the stakes are so high I feel we must be certain.
>
> I would like to operationally test all my weapons. This means the missiles should be fired, and these reentry vehicles detonated in space to make sure that the warhead will go off and to test our operational factors.[15]

If and when the Nike X antiballistic missile system is fully developed, the same logic applies with respect to full systems testing. If one wishes to be certain that all the many complex components will interact as planned, they must be fully tested with the warhead. If one wants to find out whether or not he can track, whether or not he can see, for how long he can see, and over what areas, whether he can kill the enemy warhead, and whether the second and third and fourth defense missiles are operative, then full scale testing is required. If it is not fully tested, and it cannot be under the Test Ban Treaty, there will always be doubts whether it will work as planned. Thus, under the Test Ban Treaty, it is impossible to say positively that either the land-based strategic missiles or any ABM that is developed will work as expected. To make the situation even worse, it is impossible to calculate the degree of doubt. As Dr. Teller said, it is simi-

---

[15] *Ibid.*, p. 780.

lar, only worse, because the missile is more complex, to marketing a new design of automobile without road testing it. And in this case, the national security depends upon the proper working of the machine.[16]

Yield Verification of Stockpiled Weapons

Another problem posed by a ban of atmospheric tests is that of checking stockpiled nuclear weapons from time to time to ensure that they are still in good working condition. As Dr. John Foster pointed out, nuclear weapons are "not things that can be put on the shelf and work forever without attention."[17] They require periodic examination, correction, and proof testing. The smaller weapons can be proof-checked underground, but weapons of a yield of a megaton or more would require proof testing in the atmosphere. As time goes on, and there are no proof tests, there will be more and more doubt as to whether something has deteriorated with age and will not work properly. High explosive weapons are always checked periodically, and it would seem at least as important to check stockpiled nuclear weapons.

Troop Training

Another constraint of the Test Ban Treaty is that it will render impossible troop exercises conducted with actual nuclear weapons. These are useful because they give key officers and men the experience of actually maneuvering in the vicinity of a tactical nuclear weapon blast, as they may

---

[16] For further discussion of missile reliability, *see* James H. McBride and John I. H. Eales, *Military Posture* (New York: Praeger, 1965), pp. 1–20.

[17] *Preparedness Investigating Subcommittee Hearings*, p. 400.

have to do in war. The restraint may not be serious, but it is still to some degree a disadvantage. General Wheeler evaluated the problem as follows:

> Of course, we will be unable to use our tactical nuclear weapons in troop maneuvers or training. This will have some effect. However I don't regard this as having an overriding effect.[18]

In the absence of actual nuclear explosions, simulated explosions, lectures, and training films can be employed, and these training aids will be useful, but there is no substitute for actual experience. This can no longer be had.

---

[18] *Ibid.*, p. 657.

chapter 6

MILITARY AND TECHNOLOGICAL
ADVANTAGES AND DISADVANTAGES

Throughout the hearings on the Test Ban Treaty, Administration witnesses readily admitted that the United States must maintain military superiority. All admitted that there were risks involved in the treaty from the military and technological point of view, but they maintained that these risks were small. The President, in his message to the Senate, said:

> Our choice is not between a limited treaty and effective strategic strength—we need and can have both. . . . This treaty will assure the security of the United States better than unlimited testing.[1]

A number of key witnesses, including Dr. Bradbury, Dr. Foster, Dr. Teller, General Le May, General Power, General Schriever, General Twining, General Booth, Admiral Anderson, and Admiral Burke, voiced a different opinion. For example, Dr. Bradbury said: "I don't see any technological risks in continued testing. In fact I think the military stands to gain. I can't see how they could possibly lose."[2] General Schriever said:

> . . . from a military standpoint, and being responsible for the development of the systems for the Air Force and the advancement of technology, I would say that the treaty has certain disadvantages from the standpoint of my responsibility, definitely.[3]

General Booth said that under the treaty, as Chief of Defense Atomic Support Agency, he could not meet the requirements

---

[1] *Foreign Relations Committee Hearings, op. cit.,* p. 3.
[2] *Preparedness Investigating Subcommittee Hearings,* p. 411.
[3] *Ibid.,* p. 832.

the services had placed upon him,[4] and General Twining said: "The Treaty will eventually weaken our military capacity."[5]

Each of these witnesses had made his own analysis of the advantages and disadvantages of the treaty from his own point of view, and all of them were in positions of great responsibility, but they necessarily based their conclusions on their own experience and knowledge. It is the purpose of this chapter to analyze the military and technological advantages and disadvantages of the treaty based on all the declassified information presented to both the Foreign Relations Committee and the Preparedness Investigating Subcommittee and to reach an independent conclusion as to the risks involved in the treaty. For purposes of analysis these risks can be divided into three categories: (1) direct constraints resulting from the treaty; (2) indirect constraints resulting from the treaty; and (3) other. Each category will be discussed in turn, and finally the possible advantages of the treaty will be examined.

Direct Constraints Resulting from the Treaty

Analysis of the subject material covered in Chapters III and V reveals that there are some twenty existing military requirements for nuclear testing.[6] Of these twenty requirements, thirteen cannot be met under the treaty; four can be only partially met; and three can be accomplished through underground testing, although at a greater cost in terms of money and effort. It is immediately apparent, then, that of the existing requirements for nuclear testing, only 15 per cent can be fully met under the treaty. The fact that 85 per cent

[4] *Ibid.*, p. 187.
[5] *Ibid.*, p. 970.
[6] *See* Appendix V, "Existing Requirements for Nuclear Testing."

of these requirements cannot be completely met inevitably results in military constraints that produce risks to the national security. An examination of Appendix V in light of the discussion in Chapters III and V indicates the following risks:

1. The United States will be unable to determine the ability of its hardened underground second-strike missile systems to survive a first strike.[7]

2. The United States will be unable to equal Soviet achievements in high yield technology, including effects knowledge.[8]

3. The United States will be unable to make needed studies of the radar blackout problem.[9]

4. The United States will be unable to make needed studies of the communications blackout problem.[10]

5. The United States will be unable to gain needed data concerning the vulnerability of warheads and nose cones to defensive explosions.[11]

6. The United States program for producing hardened warheads and nose cones will be impeded.[12]

7. The United States will be unable to determine precisely and confirm the lethal radius of its ABM warheads.[13]

8. The United States will be unable to produce an optimum warhead for antiballistic missiles, although a less satisfactory warhead can be produced.[14]

9. The United States program for producing a higher yield-to-weight ratio for its missile warheads will be impeded, but not precluded.[15] This constraint affects not only explosive

---

[7] See "Survivability of Hardened Missile Launch Complexes," Chapter V.

[8] See "Very High Yield," Chapter III.

[9] See "Nuclear Effects" and "Antiballistic Missiles," Chapter III.

[10] See "Nuclear Effects," Chapter III.

[11] See "Penetration," Chapter III.

[12] Ibid.

[13] See "Antiballistic Missiles," Chapter III.

[14] Ibid.

[15] See "Very High Yield" and "Intermediate Range," Chapter III.

force, but also penetration, since if weight can be reduced while yield and thrust remain constant, the savings can be utilized for additional decoys or further hardening of the nose cone.

10. The United States program for producing weapons with less fallout will be impeded in the higher yield ranges, where tests cannot be conducted underground.[16]

11. The United States will be unable to conduct full scale operational tests of any of its missiles.[17]

12. The United States will be unable to conduct operational tests of its antiballistic missile system.[18]

13. The United States will be unable to conduct yield verification tests of stockpiled weapons of over a megaton.[19]

14. The United States will be unable to conduct troop training and orientation exercises using nuclear weapons.[20]

15. The Test Ban Treaty will not preclude the Soviet Union from overcoming any lead the United States may hold in the low and intermediate yield ranges up to about five megatons.

The above fifteen risks, the results of the military and technological constraints of the treaty, are indeed impressive. But it was argued by the Foreign Relations Committee, in its report on the Test Ban Treaty, that the constraints of the treaty would apply equally to the Soviet Union and the United States.[21]

A careful analysis of the above fifteen risks in light of the state of the art would indicate that this conclusion is hardly valid. The United States appears to be much more limited

---

16 *Ibid.*

17 *See* "Missile Reliability," Chapter V.

18 *See* "Missile Reliability," Chapter V, and "Antiballistic Missiles," Chapter III.

19 *See* "Yield Verification," Chapter V.

20 *See* "Troop Training," Chapter V.

21 U.S. Congress, Senate, Foreign Relations Committee, *Report on Executive M* (The Nuclear Test Ban Treaty), 88th Cong., 1st Sess., 1963, p. 12.

by the treaty than is the Soviet Union. This can be demonstrated by briefly analyzing each of the fifteen risks.

1. *Survivability of Second Strike Missile Systems.* The Soviet Union is less constrained than the United States because it maintains a first-strike posture and has less need to concern itself with survivability, while the United States deterrent force must be able to absorb a first strike and survive in order to deter aggression. Further, the Soviets probably have more nuclear effects data than the United States and certainly have more high yield effects data; hence they may know more about United States force vulnerability than do American technicians.

2. *High Yield Technology.* The Soviet Union has a monopoly in this area, which is frozen by the Test Ban Treaty, so the constraint can hardly be said to be equal.

3. *Radar Blackout.* The degree of constraint depends upon the relative state of the art and this is an unknown factor. Since the Soviet Union has had more opportunity for obtaining information on radar blackout than the United States, it would be prudent to assume that the Test Ban Treaty freezes a situation of Soviet superiority. If this is true, then the constraint favors the Soviet Union. At best, the constraint would apply equally, but this conclusion can be reached only by a subjective combination of hoping with guessing.

4. *Communications Blackout.* The same logic applies here as in number three above.

5. *Warhead Vulnerability.* The same logic again.

6. *Hardened Warheads.* The same logic again.

7. *Lethal Radius of ABM Warhead.* The same logic again.

8. *Optimum Warhead for ABM.* The same logic again.

9. *Improvement of Yield to Weight Ratio.* The Soviet lead in the higher yield is frozen by the treaty, whereas the presumed United States lead in the lower yields is not so

protected. The United States, then, is more constrained than
is the Soviet Union.

10. *Production of Cleaner Weapons.* Both sides appear to
be similarly constrained.

11. *Operational Tests of Missiles.* The Soviet Union has
tested its missiles; therefore it is not constrained to the extent
the United States is.

12. *Operational Tests of ABM.* Both sides appear to be
similarly constrained.

13. *Yield Verification Tests.* Both sides are similarly constrained.

14. *Troop Exercises with Nuclear Weapons.* Both sides
are similarly constrained.

15. *Low and Medium Yield Weapons Development.*
Neither side is constrained up to about five megatons.

In view of this analysis it appears that the constraints of
the treaty apply equally to only five of the areas of risk, while
the United States is more severely constrained than the Soviet Union in four. In six areas there is insufficient intelligence of the Soviet state of the art to render a completely certain judgment, but the indications are that the United States
is probably more constrained than the Soviet Union because
each of the six depends upon knowledge of nuclear effects.
One must conclude, then, that the United States is more
severely constrained by the treaty than the Soviet Union is.

Indirect Constraints Resulting from the Treaty

There are three possible indirect effects of the treaty that
could seriously degrade United States military posture. These
are (1) a degradation of the confidence factor in United
States war plans compared to what that confidence factor
would have been with further testing to reduce inadequacies
in technical knowledge, (2) the impact of the ban on testing

in three environments on the laboratories, and (3) the question of future undefined problems.

Confidence Factor in the War Plans

There are always a number of uncertainties in any war plan and therefore always some degree of risk that the plan, if implemented, will not work as expected. Obviously the fewer uncertainties there are, the greater the confidence that can be placed in the plan. There will always be uncertainties about enemy plans of attack and defense as well as uncertainties concerning the capabilities and quantities of enemy offensive and defensive weapons. It is the function of intelligence to reduce these uncertainties to a minimum, but this is very difficult to do with a potential adversary like the Soviet Union, which has a closed society and a highly sophisticated security and counterintelligence system. There may also be uncertainties about one's own offensive and defensive capabilities, and this can be an even greater problem, especially when one can certainly discover, through testing, the capabilities of his own weapons. If both uncertainties exist, that is, uncertainties about enemy capabilities and uncertainties about one's own capabilities, the confidence that can be placed in the war plan's working as expected becomes rather shaky. Further, when one is faced with an adversary like the Soviet Union, whose security is so effective that there are great uncertainties about its capabilities, it is all the more important that he know his own capabilities as precisely as possible. At present there are a great many uncertainties about the United States offensive and defensive capabilities that could be resolved by testing in the atmosphere but that cannot be resolved under the restrictions of the Test Ban Treaty. A few of the more important areas of uncertainty brought out in the hearings are:

(1) The design criteria and the responsiveness of the hardened missile launch complexes. Neither has been tested.

(2) The reliability and dependability of the offensive missiles. Only the Polaris has been tested under operational conditions from launch to explosion. This leaves an incalculable degree of uncertainty as to how these weapons will perform under operational conditions.

(3) The effect of radar and communications blackout on United States defenses and command and control systems. Too little is known about this blackout problem to remove uncertainties about capabilities under combat conditions.

(4) The effectiveness, capabilities, and reliability of any ABM system the United States might deploy. Without operational, full-scale testing this information can never be learned, but can only be judged, based upon theoretical calculations and component testing.

(5) Yield verification of stock-piled nuclear weapons over about a megaton. As weapons grow older in the stockpile, they are subject to deterioration and need to be tested to determine whether they still function as designed.

The degree to which these uncertainties reduce confidence in the war plan cannot be determined, because it is simply impossible to quantify precisely the risk involved in employing untested weapons in an environment that is not fully understood. An example of such risk, however, is the classic case of the untested torpedo in World War II. The United States developed, produced, and deployed a new torpedo, but did not operationally test it. The scientists assured the military forces that it would work, but when World War II came about, and submarines armed with this torpedo were deployed against the enemy in the Pacific, it was discovered through bitter combat experience that they would not explode. There was only a small error in the fuse, which would have been discovered if the torpedo had been tested operationally, but that small error had a serious impact upon the war in the Pacific. Today, it would be infinitely more disastrous if there were some such small error in the Minuteman or in the launch complexes. Without testing one cannot be sure that this is not the case—until these systems are employed in war, and then it is too late. General Power warned the Preparedness Investigating Subcommittee of this problem, and concluded: "So it must be a proven capability. You can see the danger when you are speculating on a quality."[22]

The Impact of the Test Ban Treaty on the Laboratories

During the 1958–61 moratorium the vitality and capability of the United States nuclear laboratories seriously declined because of their enforced inactivity and lack of support.[23] President Kennedy recognized this problem, and on March 2, 1962, said:

> In actual practice, particularly in a society of free choice, we cannot keep top flight scientists concentrating on the preparation of an experiment which may or may not take place on an unstated date in the future, nor can large technical laboratories be kept fully alert on a standby basis waiting for some other nations to break an agreement.
>
> This is not merely difficult or inconvenient. We have explored this alternative thoroughly and found it impossible of execution.[24]

If the President was correct, the laboratory capability to be ready for testing in the prohibited environments at some undefined date would decay, and if the United States found it necessary to resume testing in these environments, it would

---

[22] *Preparedness Investigating Subcommittee Hearings, op. cit.,* p. 811.
[23] *See* "1961–62 Test Series," Chapter I.
[24] "Nuclear Testing and Disarmament (An Address Delivered from the White House by Radio and Television)," *Department of State Bulletin,* March 19, 1962, p. 447.

again be a long, slow, and not very effective process, as was the case after the moratorium. As Dr. Seaborg noted, however, if underground testing is vigorously pursued, the problem will be ameliorated. He testified, "I think there will be a problem in keeping the laboratories strong and keeping a sufficient number of scientists together but this will be helped because of the continuance of underground testing."[25]

Dr. John Foster, the Director of the Lawrence Radiation Laboratory, expressed his opinion on this problem in the following colloquy with Senator Saltonstall:

> DR. FOSTER: Whether or not the proposed treaty banning atmospheric tests permits the Laboratory to maintain a viable program in the future depends, one, on public opinion, because that determines in a major way whether or not the new young people come in and maintain the Laboratory; two, whether or not the Laboratory is provided an opportunity to test at yields and at rates of tests that is compatible with the requirements of the Laboratory program as envisaged by the Laboratory; and third, the question as to the details, the interpretation of the treaty.
>
> SENATOR SALTONSTALL: Those are points, but boiled down—
>
> DR. FOSTER: Regarding underground testing.
>
> SENATOR SALTONSTALL: But basically, you feel that it was wiser not to have the treaty which, in its present form, bans atmospheric tests.
>
> DR. FOSTER: I believe that it would be unwise, in my opinion. It is dangerous for the Laboratory to go ahead under the conditions spelled out in the treaty without assurances on the three factors that I have mentioned.[26]

According to Dr. Foster, then, a great deal depends upon the policy of the government. Dr. Bradbury, Director of the Los Alamos Scientific Laboratory, agreed, and warned:

---

[25] *Foreign Relations Committee Hearings, op. cit.,* p. 216.
[26] *Preparedness Investigating Subcommittee Hearings,* pp. 414–15.

". . . if testing is permitted by the treaty but cannot happen in practice, I think this would be the most serious situation which we can face from the point of view of laboratory morale."[27] The source of the anxiety of Dr. Foster and Dr. Bradbury was the restrictive policy that prevailed from January, 1960, right up to the time of the hearings. If the spirit of this 1960–63 policy were to be continued, the laboratories would be in a serious strait, but if the government were to reverse itself and permit the laboratories to test vigorously, and would take measures to support them morally and financially, the impact of the Test Ban Treaty on laboratory vitality, inventiveness, and effectiveness would be minimized. In a letter to Senators Mansfield and Dirksen dated September 10, 1963, President Kennedy indicated that it would be his policy to carry out a vigorous underground testing program and promised that "the United States will maintain a posture of readiness to resume testing in the environments prohibited by the present treaty . . . ."[28] But as Dr. Foster warned: "The words 'planned for readiness' are hollow unless they are backed up by a lot of very serious study."[29] There is a real risk that the American laboratories may be no match for those of the Soviet Union, but how great this risk is depends upon governmental policies, serious study, and the attitude of the American people.

Future Undefined Problems

Another risk presented by the treaty is that of coping with future unknowns. The United States does not know how much the Soviet Union knows about nuclear technology, nor does it know whether the Soviet scientists have discovered

---

27 *Ibid.*, p. 410.

28 *Congressional Record* (daily edition), 88th Cong., 1st Sess., September 12, 1963, p. 15915.

29 *Preparedness Investigating Subcommittee Hearings, op. cit.,* p. 418.

some breakthrough or critical information about nuclear effects that would enhance their defensive or offensive capabilities. Reinforcing this unknown is the great void in the American knowledge of nuclear effects. The state of the art is so young and so undeveloped that it is impossible even to imagine what breakthrough might be possible or what effects might be discovered and what impact these might have on national security. One can prepare for and guard against known problems, but it is very difficult, if not impossible, to cope with the unknown. As Dr. Foster told the Foreign Relations Committee:

> In being specific we can deal only with those problems which have already been identified. Of equal concern to me in the long run are those problems which have not yet been identified and that will surely arise in the future.
> The way in which the test ban would affect our relative ability to solve these future problems is impossible to anticipate. The best we can do is to extrapolate on the basis of our experience, to examine what we have felt was essential in the past.[30]

Both Dr. Foster and General Twining felt that there was a considerable chance that, because of the Soviet quantum jump in nuclear technology compared to the modest progress of the United States, the American deterrent had been degraded. Under questioning by Mr. Russell Fee, Special Consultant to the Preparedness Investigating Subcommittee, Dr. Foster said that this was the greatest danger of the treaty:

> MR. FEE: Now two general questions. What in your opinion is the greatest risk or danger which the United States would run by entering into this agreement?
> DR. FOSTER: I think the greatest danger would be for us to find out at some later date that we had, through an inferior technological capability an inferior deterrent, an inadequate

---

[30] *Foreign Relations Committee Hearings, op. cit.,* p. 613.

deterrent in the eyes of the Russians and perhaps even in fact.[31]

General Twining testified on this problem as follows:

> The military disadvantages during the moratorium have since been compounded by the known Soviet gains in present nuclear technology. Of perhaps even greater importance, the Soviets may well have made a breakthrough in nuclear technology unknown to the United States and denied to the United States under the terms of the treaty which could cause a serious shift in the balance of power.
>
> Now, to add one final thought—this treaty creates an artificial restriction on our ability to acquire and use increased knowledge of nuclear weaponry. Artificial ceilings on man's acquisition of knowledge are unnatural. The uncertainty of not knowing whether or not one is behind or losing superiority could create great international instability.[32]

The risk of the unknown is certainly serious; how serious, it is impossible to judge. One thing is clear, however: knowledge is strength, and the Test Ban Treaty is a barrier to knowledge. It is a spin of the wheel of fortune, and the Soviet Union, like the carnival huckster, may have the wheel rigged.

Other Risks and Disadvantages

In addition to the risks and disadvantages to the United States resulting from the prohibition of testing in the atmosphere, underwater and in space, there are other risks and disadvantages brought on by the treaty. These concern the Plowshare program, the risk of abrogation, the risk of clandestine testing, and the precedent that has been set on the inspection issue. Each of these will be discussed in turn.

---

[31] *Preparedness Investigating Subcommittee Hearings, op. cit.,* p. 339.
[32] *Ibid.,* p. 973.

Plowshare

Article I, Paragraph 1 of the Test Ban Treaty provides:

Each of the Parties to this Treaty undertakes to prohibit, to prevent, and not to carry out any nuclear weapon test explosion, *or any other nuclear explosion* [emphasis supplied] at any place under its jurisdiction or control. . . .

Article I, Paragraph 2, provides:

Each of the Parties to this Treaty undertakes furthermore to refrain from causing, encouraging, or in any way participating in, the carrying out of any nuclear weapon test explosion, *or any other nuclear explosion* [emphasis supplied], anywhere which would take place in any of the environments described. . . .

The underlined words, "or any other nuclear explosion," were inserted in the treaty at the insistence of the Soviet Union and were aimed directly at the United States Plowshare program. The State Department Legal Advisor explained this provision in a written opinion dated August 14, 1963:

The basis for the Moscow negotiations was the draft of the limited nuclear test ban treaty tabled in Geneva on August 27, 1962, by the United States and United Kingdom delegations. Article I of that draft prohibited nuclear weapons tests. Explosions were dealt with in Article II. Such explosions were permitted, but were to be subjected to controls because of the difficulty of distinguishing peaceful purpose explosions from weapons tests.

In the course of the Moscow negotiations, the Soviets rejected Article II of the August 1962 draft completely. This rejection would have left a loophole in the Treaty if Article I had remained confined to "nuclear weapon test explosions." A party might have conducted explosions revealing valuable military data or even weapon tests on the pretense that they were in fact peaceful purposes explosions and not "nuclear weapon test explosions." In order to close this loophole, the phrase "any other nuclear explosion" was inserted in Article I at the appropriate points. Its purpose is to prevent, in the specified environments, peacetime nuclear explosions that are not weapons tests. That is its only significance.[33]

President Kennedy mentioned the impact of the treaty on the Plowshare program in his message transmitting the treaty in the Senate on August 8, saying: "Continued research on developing the peaceful uses of atomic energy will be possible through underground testing."[34]

The President's statement is true, but he tactfully refrained from explaining how these nuclear explosives could be put to use once they are developed. The treaty provides that underground explosions may be conducted provided that radioactive debris is not transmitted beyond the territorial limits of the State under whose jurisdiction or control such explosion is conducted,[35] and this provision severely restricts the Plowshare program.

The Secretary of State's testimony before the Foreign Relations Committee would seem to indicate that he was unaware of any restrictions on Plowshare. He said:

Now, if we get to the operational aspect of peaceful uses, suppose there is a harbor to be dug, a canal to be dug, if we have perfected the technique by which, through which, we ourselves will be prepared to use nuclear explosions for peaceful purposes, then I should think it would be entirely manageable insofar as this treaty is concerned because we would not want a massive contamination of the environment or massive or large fallout going all over the landscape, and many of the peaceful purposes that I have looked into are, in fact, related

[33] *Foreign Relations Committee Hearings, op. cit.,* p. 77.
[34] *Ibid.,* p. 3.
[35] Article I, Paragraph 1(b).

to underground explosions for these major engineering projects.[36]

The facts of the problem were brought out by the scientists who direct the program, especially Dr. Seaborg, Chairman of the Atomic Energy Commission, and Dr. Foster of the Lawrence Radiation Laboratory.[37]

The Atomic Energy Commission has not yet perfected the nuclear explosives it needs for earth moving and excavation in connection with Plowshare, but this can be done in a period of a few years by conducting underground testing at the Nevada test site. But in the operational use of the developed explosives some radioactive debris will inevitably always be released into the atmosphere, and although the quantity may be very small, if it travels beyond the border of the country in which the explosion took place the treaty has been violated. If the explosion took place in the interior of a very large country, such as the United States, China, or the U.S.S.R., there is a good chance that no radioactive material would travel beyond its borders. But if the explosion took place in a small country, such as Panama, the treaty would certainly be violated. The construction of sea-level canals and harbors would be completely precluded under the treaty because (1) the explosion would have to take place right at the territorial limits of the country, and (2) some explosions would have to take place underwater, a forbidden environment.

The only way that the severe restrictions placed upon Plowshare could be removed would be to amend the treaty, yet who would believe that the Soviet Union would be willing to eliminate that portion of the treaty that it deliberately inserted to preclude nuclear explosions for peaceful pur-

36 *Foreign Relations Committee Hearings, op. cit.,* p. 26.
37 *Ibid.,* pp. 210, 211, 213, 239, 240 and 265. See also *Preparedness Investigating Subcommittee Hearings, op. cit.,* pp. 527–28.

poses? It would seem that the Soviet Union has successfully blocked American ambitions to put nuclear explosives to work for the material betterment of mankind, and unless the treaty is amended the United States will be unable to go ahead with the new canal it wants in Central America or the new harbor once planned for Alaska. The dreams of vast water reservoirs in the desert, new methods of mining and releasing oil, and a source of water for future astronauts visiting the moon would also be stillborn because of the Test Ban Treaty.[38]

Abrogation

In the light of history, it appears that the moratorium declared in 1958 was made by the Soviets to be breached. The ruse worked perfectly: the United States relaxed its vigil, the Soviet preparations for the resumption of testing went undiscovered by American intelligence, and the Soviet Union made vast gains in nuclear technology over the United States. In his speech of March 2, 1962, President Kennedy

---

[38] The following letter to the editor, signed by Arleigh A. Burke, Willard F. Libby, and Lewis L. Strauss, appeared in the *Washington Star,* January 26, 1965:

Sir: In your editorial, 'Plowshare and the Bomb' (January 16, 1965), you properly call attention to "an absurdity" in the nuclear Test Ban Treaty which prohibits us from "the relatively cheap and swift digging of a new sea-level canal between the Atlantic and Pacific oceans. . . .

When we ratified the treaty, we allowed ourselves to be placed in a position where henceforth we have to go hat in hand to the other signatories to ask their consent before we can undertake an engineering project essential not only to our commerce but to our defense. If a Sukarno, a Nasser, a Nkrumah, or any one of a hundred signatories, not to mention the Soviets, should refuse, we are bound.

Testifying before the Senate Committee on Foreign Relations in August 1963, we pointed out this pitfall and urged that we reserve the right to construct harbors, canals, and other peaceful works by the use of nuclear explosives. Spokesmen for the Government characterized various reservations suggested by us as without merit, and the Treaty was ratified as submitted.

indicated that the United States had learned its lesson. He said:

We know enough now about broken negotiations, secret preparations, and the advantages gained from a long test series never to offer again an uninspected moratorium. Some may urge us to try it again, keeping our preparations to test in a constant state of readiness. But in actual practice, particularly in a society of free choice, we cannot keep top flight scientists concentrating on the preparation of an experiment which may or may not take place on an uncertain date in the future nor can large technical laboratories be kept fully alert on a standby basis waiting for some other nation to break an agreement. This is not merely difficult or inconvenient. We have explored this alternative thoroughly and found it impossible of execution.[39]

In June, 1963, however, the United States declared a unilateral moratorium on atmospheric testing, and this was followed by the formal treaty providing for an uninspected ban on tests in three environments on August 5. The question immediately arises, can the Soviet Union again abrogate an agreement and achieve another quantum jump? Opinions presented to the Senate varied, but the Administration witnesses all stated that there was little risk involved in a second Soviet abrogation. It was admitted by both General Taylor[40] and William Foster, Chief of the Arms Control and Disarmament Agency,[41] that there was little chance that American intelligence could detect preparations for abrogation, but Secretary Rusk explained that a treaty is a more serious undertaking than a moratorium, especially a treaty signed

---

[39] "Nuclear Testing and Disarmament (Radio and Television Speech Delivered March 2, 1962)," *Department of State Bulletin,* March 19, 1962, p. 447.
[40] *Foreign Relations Committee Hearings, op. cit.,* p. 319.
[41] *Preparedness Investigating Subcommittee Hearings, op. cit.,* pp. 73–74.

by most of the nations of the world.[42] Secretary McNamara
explained why, from a military point of view, the risk of
abrogation is small, and his words are in strange contrast to
those of the President seventeen months earlier. Mr. Mc-
Namara argued:

Next, I should like to address the problem of surprise
abrogation of the treaty.

In weighing the military consequences of this treaty, we
have naturally considered the risk of sudden Soviet abrogation.

The consensus is that the Soviets could not in a single series
of tests, however carefully planned those might be, achieve a
significant or permanent lead in the strategic field, much less a
superweapon capable of neutralizing our deterrent force.

Moreover, as long as (1) we maintain the vitality of our
weapons laboratories and (2) we retain the administrative and
logistic capabilities required to conduct a test series in any
environment, the Soviets even with surprise will not be able
to achieve a significant time advantage.

Therefore, we believe that surprise abrogation does not
pose a serious threat to our national security.

We will maintain the vitality of our weapons laboratories.
We will continue to conduct a program of underground tests
as those may be necessary to meet our military requirements.
As I stated earlier, practically the complete range of weapons
development tests—with the exception of experiments with
very high yields—and some weapons effects experiments can
be carried out underground. This ongoing test program will
also include tests designed to lay the foundation for a major
atmospheric series to be conducted in case of Soviet abrogation.

The second requirement—to retain the administrative
talent and other resources required for quick expansion of our
test program into additional environments—can clearly be
met if we have the necessary will, and I think we have and
will continue to have that will. We have the determination to

---

retain a readiness to test in every relevant environment. This is a firm national policy. Its existence will not only render the risk of abrogation nominal, but will also constitute a strong deterrent to abrogation.[43]

Within a span of seventeen months the Administration apparently completely reversed its position on its ability to maintain a readiness-to-test posture. Explanation of, or reasons for, this reversal were not given.

While Administration witnesses said that the risk of abrogation did not pose a "serious threat" to national security, they did admit that the Soviet Union could make some gains through abrogation no matter how well prepared to resume testing the United States might be. Dr. Brown argued that the Soviet Union could gain some time advantage in obtaining new knowledge, but since several years are required to convert knowledge into weapons, the few months of time they would gain would not be important.[44] Dr. Foster and Dr. Teller, scientists with as much stature and experience as Dr. Brown, but without political responsibility to the Secretary of Defense, disagreed. Dr. Teller argued that if the Soviets were to develop a promising ballistic missile defense they could then suddenly abrogate the treaty to proof test the system. He said:

... if they have indeed perfected, installed, but not completely proven out their antimissile equipment, they could abrogate the treaty in a day, use the next week for 100 or 500 detonations, and if they find the results unsatisfactory they will have lost a treaty. If they find it satisfactory, they will have won the world.[45]

Dr. Foster felt that, if the Soviet Union abrogated the treaty and demonstrated an ability to test similar to that

---

[43] *Ibid.*, p. 109.
[44] *Ibid.*, pp. 551, 562.
[45] *Ibid.*, p. 468.

which they demonstrated in the 1961–62 series, the United States would again not keep pace.[46] In other words, he feared a repetition of the 1961–62 test series with a similar performance on both sides.

In sum, there does appear to be a risk of abrogation by the Soviet Union. How great this risk is would seem to depend on three factors: (1) what achievements the Soviet Union has made that it could bring to fruition through testing in the atmosphere; (2) the scope and intensity of Soviet preparations for testing; and (3) the effectiveness, intensity, and scope of United States preparations for the resumption of testing in the atmosphere. The first of these factors is unknown. As for the second, the Soviets have demonstrated tremendous capability. With respect to the third, it can only be hoped that the American future is more promising than the recent past.

Clandestine Testing

The risks involved in clandestine testing were discussed in Chapter IV. It was concluded that the Soviet Union can conduct in the atmosphere clandestine tests of some importance to their ABM program and to determining vulnerabilities of the United States hardened second strike force, but that this risk could be reduced if the United States detection system were improved. It was also concluded that the Soviet Union could conduct weapons development tests in space, but that the incentive for this activity seemed rather small.[47] The risk of clandestine testing by itself does not appear formidable, but the Soviets could make some gains and fill some gaps in their knowledge of weapons effects that, when added

---

[46] *Ibid.*, p. 617. See also *Preparedness Investigating Subcommittee Hearings, op. cit.*, p. 441.

[47] For a report on the improvement in United States detection capabilities, *see* James H. McBride and John I. H. Eales, *Military Posture: Fourteen Issues before Congress 1964* (New York: Praeger, 1965), pp. 81–94.

to their existing knowledge, could be of great value. It often requires only the addition of one tiny piece to complete a picture puzzle or a new weapons system.

Inspection

In his speech of March 2, 1962, President Kennedy said:

> We know enough now about broken negotiations, secret preparations, and the advantages gained from a long test series never to offer again an uninspected moratorium.[48]

Seventeen months after the President made this statement the Test Ban Treaty with the Soviet Union was signed. It would seem that an uninspected treaty and an uninspected moratorium might present similar dangers, abrogation and clandestine testing. But Secretary Rusk explained to the Foreign Relations Committee that a treaty was a more serious undertaking than a moratorium, and especially a treaty signed by most of the nations of the world.[49] The implication was that world opinion would react more effectively to the breach of a treaty than to a breach of a moratorium, yet, as Admiral Burke observed, the only safeguard that is really effective is the right of inspection.[50] He went on to say:

> What is lacking, from the present treaty is an element which the Soviet Union has consistently refused to provide over the entire course of our disarmament negotiations with them. I refer specifically to an absence of truly meaningful enforceability, namely, inspection.
>
> Without a system of inspections which makes it possible to enforce realistically the sincerity of stated intentions, a test ban treaty cannot lead to the results which are claimed for it. The current treaty is, in essence, a self-contradictory document. The discussions about the treaty imply a mutual sincerity

---

48 "Nuclear Testing and Disarmament," *loc. cit.*
49 *Foreign Relations Committee Hearings, op. cit.,* pp. 52–53.
50 *Preparedness Investigating Subcommittee Hearings, op. cit.,* p. 957.

of purpose and yet demand that we take proper safeguards to protect it against a lack of sincerity.

If we are to have a limited treaty which has some real meaning, then both sides must have knowledge of what is happening, and that means we must have some limited inspection. The effectiveness of the treaty is significantly weakened since there is no definite level of inspection incorporated into the treaty.[51]

The refusal of the Soviets to permit any meaningful inspection underlines their offensive posture and suggests that clandestine testing or surprise abrogation may be their real purpose; but beyond that, there is another danger. President Kennedy indicated in his American University speech of June 10, 1963, that he was searching for a détente with the Soviet Union. Six weeks later, in his address to the nation explaining the Test Ban Treaty on July 26, he described the treaty as a "first step." The question is: Could the United States, in its eagerness to seek better relations with the Soviet Union, and in its eagerness for a comprehensive test ban treaty, expand the "no inspection" principle to a comprehensive test ban treaty as a gesture of hope and faith? If this should come to pass, the stage might well be set for a massive abrogation by the Soviet Union and a quantum jump in their technology similar to the moratorium experience. This is a serious risk and one that should be recognized. It is often said that history has a habit of repeating itself, and détente and arms control appear as twin Lorelei singing sweetly to the American Siegfried.

Advantages

During the Senate hearings on the Test Ban Treaty three advantages in the military-technological field were claimed

---

[51] *Ibid.*, pp. 938–39.

for the treaty. These were: (1) the treaty will serve to pro-long United States superiority in the areas in which it is ahead of the Soviet Union; (2) the United States is unable to compete with the Soviet Union in atmospheric testing and therefore it is better to ban such tests; and (3) the United States has been unwilling to match Soviet efforts in the search for nuclear technology and therefore a test ban is advantageous. Each of these advantages will be examined.

Prolong United States Superiority

All of the key Administration witnesses, Secretary Rusk, Secretary McNamara, Dr. Seaborg, and Dr. Brown, claimed that the Test Ban Treaty would prolong American superiority longer than would a situation of unlimited testing. This argument was clearly and concisely presented to the Preparedness Investigating Subcommittee by Dr. Brown:

> In the development of small- and medium-yield weapons (where we seem to be well ahead) the Soviets can indeed make gains through underground testing; but they are much less advanced in the techniques of conducting underground tests than we, and even our progress would be more rapid and less costly if above ground.
>
> So until they catch up with us in the techniques of underground testing, which I would think would take about a year, they would be inhibited relative to us very substantially, and even after they do catch up, both sides will tend to be able to make progress somewhat more slowly or more expensively than they could if they both tested in the atmosphere, and, therefore, they would tend to catch up slowly if they are behind, as I think everyone, almost everyone believes, in this area.[52]

The interesting thing about this argument is its negative, fatalistic underpinnings. It assumes that parity in nuclear

---

[52] *Ibid.*, pp. 864–65.

technology is inevitable under conditions of unrestricted testing,[53] but since the ban on atmospheric testing slows down progress, the presumed American superiority will be prolonged a few years. When it is considered that the only area where it is widely believed that the United States is ahead of the Soviet Union is precisely that area that can be developed through underground testing, this argument can lead only to the conclusion that in a few years the Soviet Union will maintain the leads it now holds, while parity in the low and medium yield ranges will be the United States strongest position. This is indeed an unpleasant picture. Underlying this argument is a very dubious philosophy of science. It holds that there is a certain definite limit to what can be learned about nuclear technology and that both the United States and the Soviet Union will soon learn all there is to know; hence the only possible end result is parity. It is like drinking a quart of milk—when the contents are consumed, there is no more.[54] This argument is not persuasive, since the more the researcher works the more he learns, and the quest for knowledge is never-ending. If one can know all there is to know, then he is God, but both God and knowledge are infinite.

It would seem, then, that this alleged advantage is invalid because it rests on a false base. Dr. Teller's position seems more persuasive. He said:

---

[53] For example, Secretary McNamara said: "If testing continued indefinitely without limit as to test environment or size of yield, the most likely ultimate result would be technical parity between the United States and the USSR" (*Foreign Relations Committee Hearings, op. cit.,* p. 447). Secretary of State Rusk told the Senate Foreign Relations Committee: ". . . it is my impression, and I think it relates to the general nature of scientific development, that the probability is that if unlimited testing goes on, there comes into being a kind of technological standoff" (*Foreign Relations Committee Hearings, op. cit.,* p. 45).

[54] For a detailed presentation of this philosophy of science, *see* Jerome Wiesner and Herbert F. York, "National Security and the Nuclear Test Ban Treaty," *Survival,* VII, 1 (January–February, 1965), 13–21.

Finally, as to the question of parity, in a very rapidly developing field, where a lot of ingenuity can be involved, I don't see any reason to suspect that parity will be accomplished. I think the harder worker will win out, and thus far the Russians have worked much harder. . . .[55]

Admiral Burke's statement on this question was parallel to that of Dr. Teller. He declared:

The most likely situation is one of asymmetry in technical achievement, and the magnitude of this asymmetry will be a function of the degree of effort and motivation which both sides apply to their nuclear programs.[56]

It would seem that a prudent course for the United States would be to get to work and achieve superiority in nuclear technology rather than resign itself to a position of second place. This advantage of the treaty, claimed by Secretary Rusk, Secretary McNamara, Dr. Seaborg, and Dr. Brown, seen in this light, becomes a disadvantage. As Admiral Burke told the Preparedness Investigating Subcommittee:

This kind of inferiority [nuclear inferiority], in this day and age, will leave the nation which accepts it almost inevitably in a position of permanent strategic inferiority.[57]

Nuclear inferiority is, of course, an unacceptable position for the United States.

The United States Is Unable to Compete with the Soviet Union in Atmospheric Testing

In testimony before the Preparedness Investigating Subcommittee, Dr. Brown declared that the United States was "more restricted" in testing in the atmosphere than the Soviet

---

[55] *Foreign Relations Committee Hearings, op. cit.,* p. 448.
[56] *Preparedness Investigating Subcommittee Hearings, op. cit.,* p. 920.
[57] *Ibid.,* pp. 918–19.

Union, implying that competition is difficult or hopeless. He said:

> Without a test ban, as in the past, we would still be more restricted than the Soviets in the use of above-ground tests because of our lack of isolated test areas and our greater regard for the consequences of radioactive fallout.[58]

His argument is based upon two restrictions: (1) the United States lack of isolated test areas; and (2) the American attitude toward fallout. The first restriction will be discussed below, while the latter will be shown to be an unfounded psychological or emotional problem in the discussion of fallout in Chapter VIII.

The United States conducts most of its atmospheric tests and all of its high yield tests at the Pacific testing grounds. The Soviet Union conducts these types of tests on Novaya Zemlya. The question is: Is it easier for the Soviet Union to test on Novaya Zemlya than it is for the United States to test in the Pacific? Novaya Zemlya is closer to the Soviet industrial base than the Pacific testing grounds are to the American industrial base, and therefore transportation costs and times may be higher. But Novaya Zemlya has an Arctic climate, and this creates costly construction and maintenance problems and limits winter supply operations to airlift. It would seem that the difficulties with test sites, while different in nature, would be similar in magnitude. Dr. Libby probably gave as good a judgment on this matter as can be had, in reply to a question by Senator Aiken:

> SENATOR AIKEN: Well, it is easier for them to test a large weapon anyway, isn't it, on account of their having the area available in which to conduct the tests?
> DR. LIBBY: I guess so. I am a little doubtful on that point, but I guess so.[59]

---

[58] *Ibid.*, p. 865.
[59] *Foreign Relations Committee Hearings, op. cit.*, p. 651.

If the lack of isolated test areas is indeed a disadvantage for the United States, it is certainly not a very serious one, and one that at most costs a little extra time and money. This should be no barrier to the United States, because, as President Johnson said in his "Message to Congress on Defense," on January 18, 1965:

> We are the wealthiest nation in the world and the keystone of the largest alliance of free nations in history. We can, and will, spend whatever is necessary to preserve our freedom.[60]

The United States does appear, then, to have the physical, technical, and economic ability to match or better Soviet test efforts, and if it has failed to do so, the reason for such failure must be sought elsewhere.[61] This advantage to the Test Ban Treaty, then, must be rejected as of little consequence.

The United States Is Unwilling to Compete with the Soviet Union in Atmospheric Testing

Dr. John Foster, Director of the Lawrence Radiation Laboratory, felt that because of the restrictive policies of the government with respect to nuclear research, the United States could not mount a test series comparable to that which the Soviet Union could conduct. Extrapolating from past experience, he prognosticated that the Soviet Union would continue to advance its technology faster than the United States. He emphasized that it was not through any lack of capability that the United States would continue to fall behind, but because of policy. He felt that the greatest risk of continued testing would be: "Through failure to implement a program which provided equal or greater rate of progress than that being achieved by the Soviet Union, to fall behind militarily."[62]

---

60 *Washington Post,* January 19, 1965.
61 *See* "1961–62 Test Series," Chapter III.
62 *Preparedness Investigating Subcommittee Hearings, op. cit.,* p. 441.

The following exchange between Dr. Foster and Senator Thurmond illustrates Dr. Foster's position:

DR. FOSTER: Since 1945 we have tried to limit this arms race and until a few weeks ago there was no serious information indicating that the Russians felt that way. We were forced to resume testing in 1961, and yet we did it with severe restrictions, and we have not been aggressive since then.

I feel that one of the real advantages from a technical military point of view to us of the treaty is that it would prevent the Soviets from testing this fall in the atmosphere.

SENATOR THURMOND: Testing what?

DR. FOSTER: It would prevent the Soviets from testing this fall in the atmosphere. I feel that if they did test this fall in the atmosphere it would represent a series of scope and size comparable to what they have done in each of the last two years, and I do not believe that the United States would be able to mount a series for [deleted] that was much more impressive than the series we launched in the summer of 1962.

In other words, we would be a little further behind; and what the treaty will permit us to do is to reduce the relative— the discrepancy in the relative rates between the two nations.

SENATOR THURMOND: Well, as I understand, the Soviets have gained important knowledge from these recent tests, and are now ahead in the high yield, and in the development of an antimissile system, and if we are going to catch up with them in those fields or attain a superiority over them, which we prefer, then it would be necessary for us to test in the atmosphere, would it not?

DR. FOSTER: Yes, sir; but it is not simply a question of testing but having the will to run the race. . . .

My point simply is, sir, if the United States continues to make this determined effort to minimize, to limit the arms race by limiting the research on nuclear explosives and their effects on weapons systems, while the Soviets continue to accelerate their efforts, I do not see how we can maintain the superiority that we feel we should have.

SENATOR THURMOND: In other words, if we are going to try to limit the arms race while the Soviets are expanding their tests and acquiring more knowledge, then that would be a dangerous situation?

DR. FOSTER: Right, sir.

SENATOR THURMOND: And it might become more dangerous in the future if we follow such a course?

DR. FOSTER: Yes, sir.

SENATOR THURMOND: But if we went all out on testing to gain all the knowledge we can in order to regain this superiority in these fields where we are now deficient, then, would it not seem that would be the part of prudence and in the interests of our national security?

DR. FOSTER: Yes, sir; but as I indicated, that has not been the trend in recent years.

SENATOR THURMOND: I understand.

DR. FOSTER: And I have no assurance that it will be reversed in the next few months, but the Soviets could resume in the next few months, and as far as I know, conduct a series at least at the level they have done at each of the last two years.

SENATOR THURMOND: I can see the points you are making.

DR. FOSTER: So, I think there is an advantage to the treaty from this point of view and for the first time in these many years it may work.

SENATOR THURMOND: I can see the point you are making, if we do not make a supreme effort and the Soviets do, then they will continue to remain ahead of us in these fields in which we are now deficient.

However, if we should make the supreme effort, we should be able to gain the knowledge that they have already gained, and should be able to acquire superiority if we were willing to make the effort.

Is that correct?

DR. FOSTER: Yes; as I understand it.[63]

If the policy of self-abnegation that was initiated in January, 1960, and continued right up to the time of the hearings were to continue under a condition of unrestricted testing,

---

[63] *Ibid.,* pp. 512–13.

as Dr. Foster feared it would, then the Test Ban Treaty would serve the purpose of prolonging whatever areas of nuclear superiority the United States might have for a while, but the end result would certainly be inferiority to the Soviet Union. But United States policy is set in Washington, not in Moscow or Peking, and the question is, does self-abnegation in nuclear technology increase the national security when the end result can only be second place in nuclear technology? Thus, whether the Test Ban Treaty enhances national security depends upon whether the United States wishes to hold first place in nuclear technology or is willing to settle for second place. If the United States wishes to ensure the first place position it has enjoyed for almost two decades, the Test Ban Treaty is a disadvantage; but if second place is acceptable, then the treaty serves to retard the Soviet momentum toward an inevitable end. But, as has been noted above, falling behind the Soviet Union in nuclear technology holds great risk of falling behind in strategic military power. There is no question that the United States enjoys strategic military superiority now, and this is because of past technological superiority. Strategic weapons systems follow technology by a minimum period of from six to eight years, and therefore there is a risk that the Soviet Union could achieve strategic military superiority not earlier than 1968 and, given their inferior production capacity, probably somewhat later. But the United States cannot afford to risk second place and no responsible American has ever advocated accepting second place. The following colloquy between Senator Jackson and Secretary of State Dean Rusk clearly expresses the official position:

SENATOR JACKSON: Mr. Secretary, I believe you have answered this question, but I want to be sure about it: Can the United States afford a position of parity or equality with the Soviet Union in nuclear weapons technology and systems? Does the United States require for an effective deterrent a margin of safety and superiority in these matters in view of Soviet secrecy?

SECRETARY RUSK: Senator, I believe that the United States must maintain in its own security interests a very large overall nuclear superiority with respect to the Soviet Union.[64]

Summary

Upon examination, the three advantages claimed for the Test Ban Treaty from a military-technological point of view are advantages only if the United States is resigned to accepting second place in nuclear technology. But since falling behind the Soviet Union in nuclear technology carries with it the risk of falling behind in strategic military power at a later date, and this is unacceptable, the advantages claimed for the treaty are not valid.

While there are no military-technical advantages to the treaty, the analysis in this chapter has uncovered twenty-three disadvantages or risks. These are:

1. The United States will be unable to determine the ability of its hardened underground second-strike missile systems to survive a first strike.

2. The United States will be unable to equal Soviet achievements in high yield technology, including effects knowledge.

3. The United States will be unable to make needed studies of the radar blackout problem.

4. The United States will be unable to make needed studies of the communications blackout problem.

5. The United States will be unable to gain needed data concerning the vulnerability of warheads and nose cones to defensive explosions.

---

[64] *Foreign Relations Committee Hearings, op. cit.,* p. 46.

6. The United States program for producing hardened warheads and nose cones will be impeded.

7. The United States will be unable to determine precisely and confirm the lethal radius of its ABM warheads.

8. The United States will be unable to produce an optimum warhead for antiballistic missiles, although a less satisfactory warhead can be produced.

9. The United States program for producing a higher yield-to-weight ratio for its missile warheads will be impeded, but not precluded.

10. The United States program for producing weapons with less fallout will be impeded in the higher yield ranges, where tests cannot be conducted underground.

11. The United States will be unable to conduct full-scale operational tests of any of its missiles.

12. The United States will be unable to conduct operational tests of its antiballistic missile system.

13. The United States will be unable to conduct yield verification tests of stockpiled weapons of over a megaton.

14. The United States will be unable to conduct troop training and orientation exercises using nuclear weapons.

15. The Test Ban Treaty will not preclude the Soviet Union from overcoming any lead the United States may hold in the low and intermediate yield ranges up to about five megatons.

16. The Test Ban Treaty serves to constrain the United States more than it does the Soviet Union in achieving nuclear superiority.

17. The Test Ban Treaty will degrade the relative confidence factor of United States war plans.

18. The Test Ban Treaty will degrade the vigor and effectiveness of the nuclear laboratories to some degree.

19. The Test Ban Treaty inhibits American ability to cope with future unknown and undefined problems, which are bound to arise.

20. The Test Ban Treaty restricts the use of nuclear explosions for the material betterment of mankind.

21. There is a risk of clandestine testing.

22. There is a risk of surprise abrogation.

23. The Test Ban Treaty has set a precedent for future uninspected treaties, which may work to the disadvantage of the United States.

How serious are these risks? In his testimony before the Foreign Relations Committee, Secretary of Defense McNamara declared:

> Thus, the risks under the treaty are either small or under our control, and the values of the treaty are substantial even if we consider only the military area.[65]

Perhaps Secretary McNamara did not take into consideration all of the above risks, but it would appear that these risks are neither small nor "under our control." Behind most of the risks listed above is lack of needed knowledge. The only way to control ignorance is through learning, yet the Test Ban Treaty cuts off the most vital source of learning, which is atmospheric testing. As Dr. Bradbury, a proponent of the treaty, said:

> I presume the only reason the executive branch has undertaken to negotiate a treaty with the Soviets is because it envisions some sort of political advantage. It is, I think, self-evident and obvious that one's military position is enhanced by further testing.[66]

The necessarily rapid analysis of the treaty, made by the Preparedness Investigating Subcommittee based on the testimony before it, revealed nine disadvantages; the Subcommittee concluded:

---

[65] *Ibid.,* p. 109.
[66] *Preparedness Investigating Subcommittee Hearings, op. cit.,* p. 523.

From the evidence we are compelled to conclude that serious—perhaps even formidable—military and technical disadvantages to the United States will flow from the ratification of the Treaty.[67]

This chapter's more time-consuming analysis, based upon testimony before both Senate committees, uncovered twenty-three disadvantages. Thus the situation appears to be even more serious than the excellent, but necessarily hasty, analysis of the Preparedness Investigating Subcommittee concluded. Just how great the risk is cannot be foreseen, because it is the risk of living in ignorance of things we need to know. As Dr. Foster said: "You are taking a risk, and you cannot calculate it." This is the most frightening risk of all; it is a toss of the dice, a spin of the wheel of fortune, a game of Russian roulette. Further, the constraints of the treaty bear more heavily upon the United States than upon the Soviet Union, and finally, America's dream of utilizing nuclear explosive power for the material betterment of mankind must be shelved for the duration of the treaty.

President Kennedy said in his address to the nation on July 26, 1963, "Our security is not impaired by the Treaty I am discussing." This statement is the foundation of all arguments for the treaty. If the national security is not impaired, then there is little to lose in this kind of attempt to reduce tensions, since diplomatic mistakes may be repaired by military might. But the report of the Preparedness Investigating Subcommittee and this chapter's analysis show that the President's advisors may have been mistaken in their analysis. They may not have taken into consideration all of the factors and all of the opinions of experts that were expressed in the two Senate hearings, or the same euphoric bias

---

[67] U.S. Congress, Senate, Committee on Armed Services, Preparedness Investigating Subcommittee, *Interim Report on the Military Implications of the Proposed Nuclear Test Ban Treaty*, 88th Cong., 1st Sess., September 9, 1963, p. 2.

that led to the policy of self-abnegation that prevailed from January, 1960, may have influenced their conclusions. In any case, if the conclusions of this chapter's analysis are correct, then the entire logic of the treaty falls, and it becomes little more than a dangerous adventure into the unknown. The real essence of the matter was expressed by President Kennedy in his address to the nation of March 2, 1962. He said:

> If our weapons are to be more secure, more flexible in their use and more selective in their impact—if we are to be alert to new breakthroughs, to experiment with new designs—if we are to maintain our scientific momentum and leadership—then our weapons progress must not be limited to theory or to the confines of laboratories or caves.[68]

The conclusion of this chapter's analysis is that nothing has happened since March, 1962, to invalidate the President's statement.

---

[68] "Nuclear Testing and Disarmament," *op. cit.*, p. 445.

chapter 7

THE SAFEGUARDS

The disappointing experience of the moratorium, its abrogation, and the comparative rates of progress in the subsequent
test series had caused some observers, as well as officials, to
question the efficacy of American policies in maintaining the
desired degree of superiority over the Soviet Union on a
long-range basis.

Following this discouraging series of events, the United
States had suddenly negotiated and signed a test ban treaty
with the Soviet Union that held grave military and technical
risks for the national security. Something had to be done to
alert Congress and the nation to the dangerous trend and,
at the same time, avoid a head-on clash between the political
and the military-technical levels of the executive branch. The
device of proposing certain "safeguards" served this function. Members of both the Atomic Energy Commission and
the Joint Chiefs of Staff insisted upon safeguards; however,
the Joint Chiefs of Staff, in their position paper on the treaty,
predicated their approval of the treaty upon the effective
implementation of certain safeguards and thus precipitated
Congressional action. In effect, they bartered their consent to
the treaty for certain changes in policy. They said:

> If we ratify this treaty, we must conduct a vigorous under-
> ground testing program and be ready on short notice to resume
> atmospheric testing. We should strengthen our detection cap-
> abilities and maintain modern nuclear laboratory facilities and
> programs. Finally, we must not for a moment forget that
> militant Communism remains committed to the destruction
> of our society.[1]

---

[1] *Preparedness Investigating Subcommittee Hearings, op. cit.,* p. 591.
See also *Foreign Relations Committee Hearings, op. cit.,* p. 276.

This was a very important statement. Not only did it serve as a stern and timely reminder to both Congress and the Administration of the nature of international communism, it was also a direct plea to Congress to use its influence to reverse the official policies on nuclear testing and readiness. Each of the Joint Chiefs of Staff was even more emphatic on these points in his individual testimony. The following quotes demonstrate their great concern:

GENERAL TAYLOR: I would certainly say that if the leaders of our Government were indicating that they would not behave in accordance with these specific safeguards, I would be against the treaty.[2]

ADMIRAL McDONALD: General Le May stated that he felt, and many of the rest of us felt, that our test programs in the past were insufficient.
I hope, and I think, that there is a possibility that this treaty, together with the safeguards that we have laid down, will perhaps stimulate our test program.[3]

GENERAL LE MAY: I feel that we could approve this treaty if, and only if, we took the necessary insurance out to nullify some of the military disadvantages and reduce the risk to an acceptable figure.[4]

SENATOR RUSSELL: Would you approve the treaty in the absence of the safeguards being accepted and applied?
GENERAL WHEELER: I believe not, Senator.[5]

General Shoup then went on to say:

I would like to call to your attention the fact that Communism has not yet been spread by the use of nuclear weapons,

---

[2] *Ibid.,* p. 598.
[3] *Foreign Relations Committee Hearings, op. cit.,* p. 367.
[4] *Preparedness Investigating Subcommittee Hearings, op. cit.,* p. 719.
[5] *Foreign Relations Committee Hearings, op. cit.,* p. 348.

and I think a fifth safeguard is an essential one at this time and that is our efforts should be tripled against the spread of Communism by methods other than the use or the threat of nuclear weapons.[6]

It would seem that, as the nation's leading military men watched the American Siegfried on his journey, they feared that he might be distracted from his mission by the lovely and seductive twin Lorelei, disarmament and détente. The enunciation of the safeguards, especially the entreaty to remember "that militant Communism remains committed to the destruction of our society" may have been a direct reply to President Kennedy's American University speech of June 10, in which he asked the American people to "reexamine our attitude towards the Soviet Union" and declared a unilateral moratorium on atmospheric tests.[7] It was also both a warning and a plea for help directed to the Congress. Senator Jackson immediately recognized the significance of the stand of the Joint Chiefs, and decided to act. He declared:

> Speaking of treaties, I think we may need two treaties. If we adopt the treaty that is to be submitted, I think we might well have a treaty between the Congress and the executive branch as to what is going to be done under it. I am serious about this.
>
> Mr. Chairman, we just can't have people coming up making statements, saying "we will do so and so," and then that person disappears and is no longer in the Government.
>
> Someone else comes along and makes a different statement. Or a statement is made to the subcommittee, and we find, when the budget comes up, the program is not in it.[8]

To implement his "two treaties" idea, Senator Jackson, on August 14, 1963, offered a motion before the Prepared-

---

[6] *Ibid.*, p. 356.
[7] "The Strategy of Peace," *Vital Speeches,* July 15, 1963, pp. 558–61.
[8] *Preparedness Investigating Subcommittee Hearings, op. cit.,* p. 425.

ness Investigating Subcommittee requesting that the Joint
Chiefs of Staff submit as soon as possible, and in any event
prior to committee action on the treaty, a statement of the
specific requirements to implement the safeguards. The motion was unanimously approved by the subcommittee, and
subsequently by the full Armed Services Committee. Chairman Russell transmitted the Jackson motion to the Secretary of Defense on August 15 and requested a statement in
response to the motion. Both the Joint Chiefs of Staff and
the Office of the Secretary of Defense replied in letters dated
August 23, 1963. The Joint Chiefs of Staff laid down specific
criteria for meeting the first four of the five safeguards, and
the Secretary of Defense, after consulting with the Joint
Chiefs of Staff, the Atomic Energy Commission, the Central
Intelligence Agency, and the Arms Control and Disarmament Agency, gave assurances that the criteria would be met.
The safeguards and criteria set down by the Joint Chiefs of
Staff were as follows:

    A. The conduct of comprehensive, aggressive, and continuing
       underground nuclear test programs designed to add to our
       knowledge and improve our weapons in all areas of signifi-
       cance to our military posture for the future.
      1. Criteria
         a. The underground test program should be compre-
           hensive. Therefore, it should be revised to include as
           many as feasible of the objectives of the tests which
           we would otherwise do under conditions of un-
           restricted testing.
         b. The underground test program should be vigorous.
           It should proceed at a pace that will exploit to the
           fullest the capabilities of existing AEC and DOD
           weapons laboratories. If these capabilities are
           proved to be inadequate to meet established re-
           quirements, they should be expanded.
         c. The underground test program should be a continu-

        ing program designed to insure the highest practicable rate of progress in nuclear technology.

    d. The standards established governing the type and magnitude of tests to be conducted should not be more restrictive than the spirit of the treaty limitations.

B. The maintenance of modern nuclear laboratory facilities and programs in theoretical and exploratory nuclear technology which will attract, retain and insure the continued application of our human scientific resources to these programs on which continued progress in nuclear technology depends.

    1. Criteria

        a. Adequate AEC and DOD budgets, modern facilities, and positive personnel policies should be maintained and augmented as necessary in order to attract and retain competent scientists in nuclear and related fields.

        b. Broad and forward-looking research programs should be carried on which will attract and retain able and imaginative personnel capable of insuring the highest practicable rate of progress that can be attained in all avenues of potential value to our offensive and defensive posture.

C. The maintenance of the facilities and resources necessary to institute promptly nuclear tests in the atmosphere should they be deemed essential to our national security or should the treaty or any of its terms be abrogated by the Soviet Union.

    1. Criteria

        a. The readiness-to-test program should be established on a governmentwide basis in support of a plan common to all participating agencies. The required resources and facilities should be maintained in a state of readiness, or earmarked, so that plans can be implemented within the reaction times established.

b. Reaction times for resumption of testing in the prohibited environments must be established and maintained within the constraints of military requirements and reasonable costs. Reaction times will vary for the broad categories of testing. As an immediate objective, we should be able to conduct proof tests of weapons in stockpile in about 2 months; operational systems tests in about 2 to 3 months; weapon developments tests in about 3 months; and weapon effects tests in about 6 months.

c. There must be provision for periodic updating of our test program plan and for checking our readiness to test.

D. The improvement of our capability, within feasible and practical limits, to monitor the terms of the treaty, to detect violations, and to maintain our knowledge of Sino-Soviet nuclear activity, capabilities, and achievements.

1. Criteria

a. The current capability of the United States to detect and identify nuclear tests conducted by the Sino-Soviet bloc must be improved to the extent it is both feasible and remunerative. (Specific proposals for this purpose are currently under consideration.)

b. A vigorous research and development program must be pursued in order to improve equipments and techniques for nuclear test detection and identification.

c. Conventional intelligence sources must continue to complement the scientific intelligence techniques.[9]

The letter from the Office of the Secretary of Defense called attention to statements by the President, the Secretary of Defense, the Secretary of State, and the Chairman of the Atomic Energy Commission, all promising to carry out the safeguards. It went on to spell out in detail just how the

---

[9] U.S. Congress, Senate, Committee on Armed Services, Preparedness Investigating Subcommittee, *Interim Report on the Military Implications of the Proposed Nuclear Test Ban Treaty*, 88th Cong., 1st Sess., September 9, 1963, pp. 23–24.

criteria would be met.[10] There could be no doubt that the Administration was now completely committed, to Congress and to the nation, to implement a new policy. Carrying the matter one step further, the Preparedness Investigating Subcommittee assumed responsibility for monitoring the implementation of the safeguards. In its report to the Senate dated September 9, 1963, it said:

> The administration has expressed publicly its intent regarding the safeguards both in the responses to the motion by Senator Jackson and in other statements by the President, the Secretary of State, and the Secretary of Defense.
>
> To permit the U.S. Senate to monitor the treaty safeguards it is necessary that the expressed good intentions be supplemented by definitive programs against which progress can be compared. If the treaty is ratified it is the intention of the Preparedness Investigating Subcommittee to monitor the implementation of the safeguards.[11]

The subcommittee did monitor the implementation of the safeguards, and on September 11, 1964, Senator Stennis, Chairman of the subcommittee, rendered a verbal report to the Senate.[12] He reported that all of the safeguards had thus far been effectively implemented with one exception, that of underground tests for gaining knowledge of nuclear effects. In the year since the treaty was signed he reported that not a single effects test had been conducted. Underground effects tests are difficult and expensive to mount, and very little information can be gained from underground testing at best. This failure, then, serves to underscore the constraints of the Test Ban Treaty. It is interesting to note that responsibility for effects testing lies with the Secretary of Defense, whose

---

10 *See* Appendix VI.

11 *Interim Report on the Military Implications of the Proposed Nuclear Test Ban Treaty, op. cit.,* p. 10.

12 *Congressional Record* (daily edition), 88th Cong., 2d Sess., September 11, 1964, pp. 21343–45.

official position had been that much could be learned about silo vulnerability through underground testing.

While the safeguards were, and continue to be, a useful tool for influencing official policies toward testing and readiness posture, they have very little impact on the twenty-three risks enumerated in Chapter VI. They serve only to ameliorate, but not eliminate, three risks: the risk of abrogation, the risk of clandestine testing, and the risk of laboratory decay. They have absolutely no impact on the other twenty risks; thus, no matter how vigorously the safeguards are pursued, the Test Ban Treaty would appear to be a very dangerous and risky adventure in international relations. This conclusion renders the Joint Chiefs of Staff's fifth safeguard, which did not lend itself to formalization, even more important. It was "not to forget for a moment that militant Communism remains committed to the destruction of our society." If this safeguard is to be implemented, the natural temptation to pursue the twin Lorelei recklessly must be tempered by conscious reason, firm knowledge, sound judgment, and, above all, an effective, integrated strategy. This is the key safeguard and the one that, if implemented, will automatically carry the others in its wake. The current American dilemma in Vietnam demonstrates both the importance of this safeguard and the complexity of its implementation. Fortunately, however, the American stand in Vietnam clearly shows that this safeguard has not been forgotten in spite of pressure from the United Nations and many other nations of the Free World and the temptations of the twin Lorelei to depart from a sound strategy.

chapter 8

POLITICAL ASPECTS

A careful reading of President Kennedy's address to the nation concerning the Test Ban Treaty[1] and his message transmitting the treaty to the Senate[2] indicates that he did not claim that the Test Ban Treaty would produce, in and of itself, any great political advantages for the United States. Rather he spoke of it as a "symbol," a "hopeful step," a "limited step," "an opportunity to reduce tension," and "an opening wedge." In short, he seemed to believe that while the treaty itself accomplished little in the political arena, it might act as a catalytic agent to precipitate further areas of agreement that may lead toward ultimate stability and peace. But he was careful to state that the treaty was "no cause for complacency," and that Soviet "nuclear and conventional arms still must be deterred." He warned: "Nothing could more greatly damage our cause than if we and our allies were to believe that peace has already been achieved and that our strength and unity were no longer required." In both of these messages, his two major statements on the treaty, he was careful to point out the limitations of the treaty. The President specifically called attention to the following thirteen limitations:

1. The treaty permits continued underground testing.
2. Any nation which signs the treaty may withdraw from it upon three months' notice.
3. The treaty is not an end to the threat of nuclear war.

---

[1] "The Test Ban Treaty: A Step Toward Peace (Address to the Nation on July 26, 1963)," *Department of State Bulletin*, August 12, 1963, pp. 234–39.

[2] "Transcript of President Kennedy's Treaty Message to the Senate," *Congressional Quarterly Weekly Report*, August 16, 1963, pp. 1457–58.

4. It will not reduce nuclear stockpiles.

5. It will not halt the production of nuclear weapons.

6. It will not restrict their use in time of war.

7. It reflects no concessions by the Soviet Union.

8. It will not resolve all conflicts, or cause the Communists to forego their ambitions, or eliminate the dangers of war.

9. It will not reduce our need for arms or allies or programs of assistance to others.

10. The Moscow talks reached no agreement on any other subject.

11. The Soviet Government is still unwilling to accept inspection.

12. No one can predict with certainty what future agreements, *if any,* can be built on the foundations of this one (emphasis supplied).

13. The familiar contest between choice and coercion, the familiar places of danger and conflict are still there (Berlin, the Congo, Cuba, Vietnam and German reunification, for example).

The President also recognized that the conflict with communism is real, and that the basis of the conflict goes much deeper than mere nationalism, to the very roots of a philosophy of man and the State. He outlined his views of this basic conflict in an address to the United Nations on September 20, 1963, while the Senate was still debating the Test Ban Treaty. He told the General Assembly:

Our conflicts are real, to be sure. Our concepts of the world are different. No service is performed by failing to make clear our disagreements. A central difference is the belief of the American people in self-determination of all people.

We believe that the people of Germany and Berlin must be free to reunite their capitol and their country.

We believe that the people of Cuba must be free to secure the fruits of the revolution that have been betrayed from within and exploited from without.

In short, we believe that all the world—in Eastern Europe

as well as Western, in Southern Africa as well as in Northern, in old nations as well as new—that people must be free to choose their own future, without discrimination or dictation, without coercion or subversion.

These are the basic differences between the Soviet Union and the United States, and they cannot be concealed. So long as they exist, they set limits to agreement, and they forbid the relaxation of our vigilance. Our defense around the world will be maintained for the protection of freedom—and our determination to safeguard that freedom will measure up to any threat or challenge.[3]

Recognizing the limited nature of the treaty and the deep basic conflict with the Soviet Union, which, he said, "sets limits to agreement," he outlined four political advantages that, he said, may be derived from the Test Ban Treaty and that were the American motivation for the treaty. These were:

First, this treaty can be a step toward reduced world tensions and broader areas of agreement.[4]

Second, the treaty can be a step freeing the world from fears and dangers of radioactive fallout.[5]

Third, this treaty can be a step toward preventing the spread of nuclear weapons to nations not now possessing them.[6]

Fourth, and finally, this treaty can limit the nuclear arms race in ways, which, on balance, will strengthen our nation's security far more than the continuation of unrestricted testing.[7]

These four possible advantages were the only positive

---

[3] "Transcript of President Kennedy's Address to the United Nations," *Congressional Quarterly Weekly Report,* September 27, 1963, p. 1692.
[4] "The Test Ban Treaty: A Step Toward Peace," *op. cit.,* p. 234.
[5] *Ibid.*
[6] *Ibid.,* p. 235.
[7] *Ibid.*

claims for the treaty made by the President. These, then, are the political advantages that must be weighed against the military and technological disadvantages enumerated in Chapter VI above. Each of these will be discussed in turn.

Reduced World Tensions

As noted above, President Kennedy told the American people in his nationwide address of July 26 that the Test Ban Treaty "can be a step toward reducing world tensions and broader areas of agreement,"[8] but he also said that he could not predict "what future agreement, if any, can be built on the foundations of this one."[9] From the American point of view, then, the importance of the treaty, in the area of tension reduction, was its function as a symbolic act of agreement, a kind of hopeful pump-priming. Tensions between the United States and the Soviet Union have been high because of continuous Soviet and Soviet-inspired acts of aggression and subversion. The United States is committed to protect and preserve the Free World, while the Soviet Union is committed to destroy all non-Communist systems with the aim of eventually bringing the entire world under Communist rule. Secretary of State Rusk also called attention to this basic conflict as the cause of tension, and he further stated that there had been no change in the purpose of the Communist movement. He told the Foreign Relations Committee: "The values that are the heritage of a free society have been menaced by a Communist bloc armed with the most modern weapons and intent upon world domination."[10] "We are still engaged in a contest between free choice and coercion,"[11]

---

8 *Ibid.*, p. 234.
9 *Ibid.*
10 *Foreign Relations Committee Hearings, op. cit.*, p. 12.
11 *Ibid.*, p. 18.

he said. He also declared that "the Soviet Union is not prepared to trust the United States, nor is the United States prepared to trust the Soviet Union."[12] No official witness testifying before the two Senate committees indicated any direct way in which the Test Ban Treaty would serve to relieve the substance of tensions or remove the cause of them. The most positive argument advanced was put forth by Secretary Rusk in the form of three indirect and oblique points. These were:

> We ought to keep open the possibility of finding particular points of agreement in the hope that if those can be achieved, it might reduce the fever somewhat. . . .[13]

> The most important thing about the treaty is what it may symbolize and what paths it may open. That, no one can now foretell.[14]

> . . . the treaty should provide us quite an opportunity to test the sincerity of Soviet protestations about their desire to explore more sweeping arrangements for preserving the peace.[15]

Obviously, from the official United States point of view, the treaty was an agreement for the sake of an agreement— a symbolic act to show that agreements were possible in the hope of encouraging more, but this treaty admittedly had nothing to do with areas of tension and removed no cause of tension. It is difficult to understand, then, how the Test Ban Treaty can do any more than create a fleeting illusion of détente, which may tend to create the dangerous atmosphere of euphoria in the American public that the President, the Secretary of State, and the Joint Chiefs of Staff warned against.

In testimony before the Senate Foreign Relations Committee Dr. Robert Strausz-Hupé, Director of the Foreign

---

12 *Ibid.*, pp. 80–81.
13 *Ibid.*, p. 21.
14 *Ibid.*, p. 20.
15 *Ibid.*, p. 109.

Policy Research Institute, rejected the use of a "symbolic act" as a means to reduce tensions. He said:

> The treaty does not bear upon the substantive issues which divide the United States and the U.S.S.R. Thus the conclusion of the treaty signifies a symbolic act which endows an existing condition with moral-legal sanction. In diplomatic history, symbolic acts of this kind which precede an understanding on concrete issues, have been proven empty of positive beneficial consequences. It would have been better diplomacy to seek agreement on such concrete issues as, for example, Berlin, Cuba, and Laos, and to cap the concrete achievement with a symbolic act.
>
> The claims staked out for the treaty by its makers appear, in view of the treaty's modest substantive content, exorbitant. The judgments of history are exceedingly slow in the making. It seems unduly hasty to seek to anticipate a verdict which history cannot give before several decades have gone by. The immoderate statements intended to dispel doubt about speedy ratification of the treaty have created an atmosphere which does not favor the prudent and sober deliberation of the provisions of the treaty.[16]

The testimony of Professor Marshall D. Shulman, a leading expert on Soviet and Communist affairs and a member of the faculty at Harvard University, also stood in contradiction to the Administration's technique of "pump-priming" as a device to cause changes in Soviet foreign policy. He told the Foreign Relations Committee:

> One of the lessons to be gained from a study of Soviet policy since the war is a realization that there is a substantial amount of interaction between Soviet policy and our own, and that the condition which has most favored the evolution of Soviet policy in the direction of moderation has been a firm resistance to Soviet probes, combined with demonstrated

---

[16] *Ibid.*, pp. 507–8.

political and economic vitality on the part of the non-Communist nations.[17]

If Professors Shulman and Strausz-Hupé, both highly respected scholars, are correct, then the Test Ban Treaty as a "symbolic act," and "opening wedge," and "an opportunity to reduce tension" was a mistake, and, in fact, may serve to whet the Soviet appetite for aggression. It would seem that a more prudent course would have been to seek agreement on some substantive area of tension, such as Cuba or Berlin, while clearly demonstrating Western political, economic, and military superiority. At least, if the actual Western superiority in these areas is clearly demonstrated to the world and Soviet aggression is firmly resisted at every point, Communist prestige cannot fail to wane and the patient, unwavering pursuit of such a firm but peaceful policy on a long-range basis would serve to discredit communism as a useful social and political system. Ultimately such a policy, which appears to be easily within American and Free World capabilities, could not fail to rob communism of its vitality and momentum and force it into decline or evolution away from its more aggressive tendencies.

The thinking behind the Test Ban Treaty seems diametrically opposed to this proposition and tends to offer respectability and the appearance of undeserved vitality to a system that in reality cannot compete with the Western-liberal system of the United States and Europe and Japan. It would seem that if the Test Ban Treaty is a symbol of anything, it is a symbol of the "easier wrong" as opposed to the "harder right," yet the "harder right" cannot be avoided until communism loses its vitality or changes its goals. These goals are not likely to be modified so long as they appear attainable, and vitality will not disappear so long as aggression appears to be feasible and profitable.

---

[17] *Ibid.,* p. 799.

While the Test Ban Treaty as a tension-reducing device has been shown to be of doubtful value to the United States and the cause of the Free World, it can be shown that it may be of great value to the Soviet Union and the cause of international communism. In the past, the Soviets have alternately produced tensions and détente as needed to advance their own interests in the pursuit of communist goals. At present, however, they have a number of problems that need attention, and Western pressure would hinder the resolution of these troubles. They therefore find an atmosphere of détente with the West useful as a means of insurance against pressure with which they are presently in a poor position to cope.

Their current difficulties include:

1. shortcomings in the economy, especially in agriculture and the chemical industry;

2. disruption within the party involving extensive reshuffling of economic administration positions and the second level of leaders, who may be involved in the succession problem;

3. difficulties between the regime and Soviet intellectuals and artists;

4. the Sino-Soviet dispute on war;

5. the effects of de-Stalinization and the resultant economic strains and political tensions with the East European satellites;

6. the trend toward nationalism and self-reliance in the West European Communist parties;

7. the lack of revolutionary prospects in the advanced industrial parts of the world, such as North America, Europe, and Japan; and

8. a lack of pliancy in some leaders of new nations in Asia and Africa—while these leaders are far from pro-Western, they often have not played the transitory role the Soviet Union expected of them.

In view of these current problems, Professor Shulman explained that the Soviet leaders plan to use the temporary relaxation of tensions as a means to further their long-range goals:

> In the perspective of another 5, 10, or 15 years, it is argued [by the Soviets] the political face of Europe may be totally changed, and may be more responsive to Soviet approaches; competitive conflicts within the Western bloc may make Japan more approachable; the Soviet economy will have overcome its difficulties and forged ahead, in contrast to the stagnation anticipated for the United States and Great Britain.
>
> Then, by a combination of political and economic means against a background of an improved power position, the Soviet Union will emerge ascendant.[18]

The functions of the effort to reduce the atmosphere of tension with the West appear to be the following:

(a) to insure against Western pressures in this period;

(b) to encourage the flowering of divisive issues in the West, particularly the conflicts between the United States and France on the one hand and the United States and Germany on the other, since this process of fragmentation has always been encouraged by the absence of an external threat;

(c) to remove the stimulus for further Western military appropriations, and a reduction in the level of Western military mobilization;

(d) to create an atmosphere which would inhibit the Western reliance upon nuclear weapons, beyond the terms of the treaty (this is illustrated by the recent Soviet protests against United States underground testing and the transfer of nuclear warheads to Canadian territory as "contrary to the spirit of the treaty");

(e) optimally, in the atmosphere of détente, or relaxation of tensions, to seek such political gains as an explicit acceptance by the United States of the Soviet position in Eastern Europe, or a reorientation of West German policy toward a

---

[18] *Ibid.,* p. 794.

less firm commitment to the West; further, in the atmosphere of reduced tensions, to encourage the installation of governments in Western Europe which would be more favorably disposed toward trade and political relations with Moscow, particularly if the United States appeared to be moving toward bilateral settlements with the Soviet Union.[19]

Indeed, the Test Ban Treaty was intended by both the United States and the Soviet Union to reduce surface tensions superficially without affecting the substance of the tensions. But far from reflecting a mutuality of interest, the coincidental mutual desire for détente reflects only differing strategies. As Dr. Strausz-Hupé pointed out, the American approach is of questionable value, whereas Dr. Shulman has shown the Soviet approach to be the hard-headed Leninist technique of the *peredyshka*—the breathing space— needed to consolidate forces for a renewed drive at the appropriate time. The Test Ban Treaty as a device for a reduction of tensions may have played directly into the Soviets' hands and given them the *peredyshka* they need to consolidate and strengthen their power position for a renewed drive at the opportune time. This policy, far from moderating Soviet policies and goals, may well serve only to increase their tempo and intensity, which is the exact opposite of the effect hoped for by the American advocates of the treaty.

The Fallout Problem

The second advantage claimed for the Test Ban Treaty was that it "can be a step freeing the world from fears and dangers of radioactive fallout."[20] It is certainly true that many people in the United States and throughout the world

---

19 *Ibid.*, p. 796.
20 "The Test Ban Treaty: A Step Toward Peace," *op. cit.*, p. 234.

are fearful that radioactive fallout will cause widespread bone cancer, leukemia, birth defects and mutations, and all sorts of mysterious maladies. Even in a society as advanced and sophisticated as the United States, fear of fallout has become a nuclear-age fetish. To a large degree this fear has been encouraged by the Communist powers in hopes that the pressure of world opinion against nuclear testing would have an impact upon United States defense policies, but unfortunately some politicians in the United States have also encouraged that fear, or at least gone along with it, rather than face the tide of misinformed opinion. During the Foreign Relations Committee hearings on the treaty Senator Russell observed: "Some of our practicing politicians have been predicating their vote on this treaty on what they call very cynically and irreverently 'the mother vote'. . . ."[21] A reading of the eighty-odd speeches made on the Senate floor during the debate on the Test Ban Treaty would indicate that Senator Russell did not exaggerate. But it is true that the Test Ban Treaty offers one way to quiet the fears of misinformed or uninformed people. Perhaps a preferred method, however, which would involve no politics and no risks to national security, would be simply to tell the public the truth about radioactive fallout, insofar as it is known. In view of the widespread alarm about fallout, which in some cases has become so acute that mothers have refused their children fresh milk, it is indeed disappointing that no official White Paper has been published by the United States government to inform the people fully and thus protect children from such rash and irrational reactions.

In both the Foreign Relations Committee hearings and the Preparedness Investigating Subcommittee hearings, government scientists were unable to support the President and the Secretary of State on the fallout question. Dr. Glenn T.

---

[21] *Foreign Relations Committee Hearings, op. cit.,* p. 214.

Seaborg, Chairman of the Atomic Energy Commission, said: ". . . I don't think this [fallout] is one of the major reasons for this treaty."[22] Dr. John Foster, Director of the Lawrence Radiation Laboratory, said: ". . . from the technical point of view I believe it [the fallout question] has no bearing on the major issue."[23] He went on to say that the argument that the Test Ban Treaty would protect the human race from the dangers of fallout could come back to haunt us, but not as a result of scientific fact.[24] Dr. Norris E. Bradbury, Director of the Los Alamos Scientific Laboratory, was even more specific than Dr. Foster. He declared:

. . . I regret that fallout from atmospheric testing has been so played up rather recently in public statements. I think this is an exaggerated situation far beyond the needs of the actual situation. . . .

I infer that some of the words which the President has used may arise to haunt us if we return to atmospheric testings, not because they are true, but because they have been said.[25]

And Dr. Edward Teller said, with characteristic frankness: "I claim these two questions, the test ban and the fallout, are linked only by propaganda."[26]

These key government scientists (Dr. Seaborg, Dr. Foster, Dr. Bradbury, and Dr. Teller) gave the two committees holding hearings on the Test Ban Treaty sufficient information on the danger of fallout from nuclear testing to eliminate the fallout question as a major argument for the treaty completely. A brief discussion of the dangers of fallout will serve to bring out the main points made by these scientists, who are, or recently have been, the key scientific figures in the de-

22 *Ibid.*, p. 243.
23 *Ibid.*, p. 622.
24 *Ibid.*
25 *Preparedness Investigating Subcommittee Hearings, op. cit.*, p. 470.
26 *Foreign Relations Committee Hearings, op. cit.*, p. 455.

velopment of nuclear technology for the United States government.

Japanese doctors who survived the atomic blasts at Nagasaki and Hiroshima told of the effects of radiation sickness and of death caused by nuclear radiation. Subsequent studies of the effects of heavy doses of intense radiation, based primarily upon the cases of Nagasaki and Hiroshima, have established that lethal doses of radiation will occur in the close proximity of nuclear explosions. This is generally understood, as is the fact that nuclear war will sprinkle large areas with lethal or damaging doses of radiation. But until March 15, 1954, there was little fear that nuclear testing could be dangerous. On that date the United States detonated a multi-megaton hydrogen bomb at Bikini Island, and an unexpectedly heavy blanket of radioactive fallout covered seven thousand square miles of the Pacific, including some inhabited islands. Natives of the islands and a few Americans at a weather station were subjected to severe doses of local fallout, but even though evacuation and treatment were slow, none of the victims died, nor did any contract leukemia or bone cancer. The incident was an accident caused by a lack of understanding of local fallout. Concerning this incident, Dr. Seaborg told the Foreign Relations Committee:

This is what we call local fallout, that is in the immediate area of the tests. The local fallout is so well understood today that this would never be repeated in a weapons test situation, and that, of course, is the only situation in which local fallout would be a problem in a testing, in a peacetime situation.[27]

As a result of this accident panic spread from Japan all over the Far East and eventually all over the world. Communist radios and publications harped intensively on the subject for months, casting the United States in the role of a cruel and sinister villain. Their cry was also taken up by

---

[27] *Ibid.*, p. 223.

respected statesmen, such as India's Prime Minister Nehru. The upshot was that worldwide fallout from nuclear tests was suddenly equated, in the public mind, with local fallout and fallout from nuclear war, and unfortunately the American government did not dispel the panic with an information campaign of truth. The irrational fear of fallout from nuclear tests grew and gained momentum until it became a major force throughout the world, yet all this could have been nipped in the bud with one of the best psychological weapons known to man—truth.

Succumbing to fear and rumor, people tend to lose sight of the fact that radiation is not an unnatural hazard to life. The natural radiation background of the biosphere has been with the earth since the beginning of time. Its distribution around the world is not uniform, but varies from place to place: its intensity is greater at higher altitudes and, of course, in areas where there is considerable radioactive material in the soil, yet there is no recorded instance in history where there has been any disease, malady, or death attributed to this natural radiation. Living in a brick house increases the radiation to which its inhabitants are exposed by a factor of about twenty times that of worldwide fallout, while the exposure of the wearer of a luminous-dial wristwatch is greater by a factor of about ten.[28] Dental and medical X-rays also expose modern man to sharply increased dosages of radiation. Surely there are many people who live in brick houses at high altitudes in an area containing considerable amount of radioactive material in the soil, wear luminous-dial wristwatches, and have dental and medical X-rays regularly, yet who fear or receive no ill effects from radiation.

In contrast to the sharp increases of radiation one

---

[28] Earl H. Voss, *Nuclear Ambush: The Test Ban Trap* (Chicago: Henry Regnery Company, 1963), p. 22.

may be exposed to by living in a brick house, wearing a luminous-dial wristwatch, living at high altitudes or in an area with considerable radioactivity in the soil, scientists agree that the total amount of radioactivity in the biosphere that has resulted from nuclear testing since the first bomb was tested at Alamogordo is about 5 per cent of the radioactivity experienced by people living in the developed industrial parts of the world, and about 10 per cent of the radioactivity experienced by the population of the world generally.[29] Dr. John Foster told the Foreign Relations Committee that the fallout from all past nuclear tests "would be something like the same thing as deciding to live a few hundred feet higher up."[30] Dr. Bradbury presented an even more graphic comparison to the Preparedness Investigating Subcommittee; he said:

> Even if the United States tested again as much as it has in the past and added the two together, it would not amount to as much radiation exposure on a world-wide basis as one would receive from spending a summer vacation in the high Rockies.[31]

Based upon the above discussion, it would seem that if one were really worried about the danger to health from radiation, it would be only logical that he should be much more concerned about the greater danger of living in brick houses or at high altitudes, such as Denver, Colorado, vacationing in the mountains, wearing luminous-dial wristwatches, or having chest and dental X-rays than about the worldwide fallout from nuclear testing. If national policy concerning nuclear tests is going to be influenced by speculation on the possible hazards of nuclear fallout, should not there also be national policies about building brick houses, or inhabiting

---

[29] *Foreign Relations Committee Hearings, op. cit.*, p. 685.
[30] *Ibid.*, p. 622.
[31] *Preparedness Investigating Subcommittee Hearings, op. cit.*, p. 495.

parts of the nation above a certain altitude, and otherwise reducing the presumed hazards of radiation? But it might be better to postpone policy decisions until scientists have determined just what the effects of radiation are on the human body. At the present stage of research in the field, some believe that it causes leukemia, bone cancer, abnormal growths, and mutations, but as yet there is no proof. Others believe that radiation is essential to life, lengthens the life span, and is responsible for the evolution from lower to higher forms of life. They also cannot yet offer proof.[32] Whatever the effects of radiation might be, worldwide fallout from nuclear tests is a very minor factor in a number of other variables that can be regulated if, after living with radiation from the beginning of time, regulation appears to be advisable. But at any rate, the inclusion of the reduction of worldwide fallout as one of the four major benefits of the Test Ban Treaty at this time seems hardly justified. In fact, such arguments would seem to intensify the effect of rumors, superstitions, and Communist propaganda, and may do real damage. A more appropriate course of action with respect to the fallout problem would seem to be to issue and widely publicize a White Paper explaining to the people the real facts of the matter, in order that their anxiety be quieted and that they be able to face the problems of life armed with better knowledge of their environment.

Nuclear Proliferation

The third advantage claimed for the treaty was that it could be a step toward preventing the spread of nuclear weapons to nations not now possessing them. The United States

---

[32] For an excellent discussion of the possible biological effects of radiation, see Voss, op. cit., pp. 3–25. See also "Could Nuclear Tests Be Good for You," Washington Star, January 2, 1965.

government has always been, and continues to be, firmly opposed to nuclear proliferation. This is not a controversial stand. There has been no question that if Egypt's Nasser, Indonesia's Sukarno, Cuba's Castro, or any one of a number of the world's more aggressive rulers were to acquire even a small nuclear capability, it would have a dangerously destabilizing effect upon international relations. The case against proliferation was well represented by President Kennedy in his March 21, 1963, press conference. He said:

> The reason why we keep moving and working on this question, taking up a good deal of energy and effort, is because personally I am haunted by the feeling that by 1970, unless we are successful, there may be 10 nuclear powers instead of 4, and by 1975, 15 or 20. With all the history of war—and the human race's history unfortunately has been a good deal more war than peace—with nuclear weapons distributed all through the world, and available, and the strong reluctance of any people to accept defeat, I see possibility in the 1970's of the President of the United States having to face a world in which 15 or 20 nations may have these weapons. I regard that as the greatest possible danger and hazard.[33]

Certainly it is desirable to preclude the further proliferation of nuclear weapons, and it is generally agreed that a number of nations beyond the current five nuclear powers have the capability of developing their own nuclear weapons within a few years. This capability stems from the possession of nuclear reactors constructed for the purpose of generating electricity because a by-product of these reactors is plutonium, the material needed for constructing nuclear weapons. Ironically, the United States has provided over forty nations with nuclear reactors under the Atoms for Peace plan, and although most of the agreements have provided

---

[33] "Transcript of President Kennedy's March 21 Press Conference," *Congressional Quarterly Weekly Report,* March 22, 1963, p. 456.

for United States inspection to preclude the stockpiling of plutonium, it is generally agreed that a determined nation can circumvent these safeguards. Thus, there is concern that the Atoms for Peace plan may actually provide some nations with atoms for war. This situation strikingly illustrates the ancient truism that tools *per se* are neither good nor bad, but in the hands of man they can be put to either good or evil uses.

The question at hand is: Since the possibility of proliferation exists, what effect will the Test Ban Treaty have upon this threat to stability and peace? Secretary of Defense McNamara correctly stated: "The treaty does not cover the subject of proliferation."[34] Nevertheless, the treaty does have some effect. Article I, Paragraph 1, of the treaty prohibits all parties to the treaty from conducting tests in the atmosphere, underwater, and in space. Paragraph 2 of the same article prohibits all parties from "causing, encouraging, or in any way participating in" the conduct of any such tests. This provision would preclude the United States, Great Britain, and the U.S.S.R. from assisting any nation in any way with testing in the prohibited environments. Thus, if a party to the treaty, not now a nuclear power, wishes to develop a nuclear capability, it must test its devices underground. The impact on nations not a party to the treaty is that parties to the treaty are forbidden to assist them with testing in the prohibited environments, although assistance in underground testing is not forbidden. But development of its own nuclear capability is only one way that a nation may acquire nuclear weapons. There is nothing in the treaty to preclude any party from selling, transferring, or giving nuclear weapons, either offensive or defensive, to any nation so long as those weapons were intended for war and not for testing. Further, two of the five current nuclear powers, China and France, did

---

34 *Foreign Relations Committee Hearings,* p. 189.

not adhere to the treaty and are free to do as they please. But even if a non-nuclear power were a party to the treaty, abided by its provisions meticulously, and received no assistance at all, the treaty would present no great obstacle to its becoming a nuclear power if it had the reactor required to produce plutonium. In his role as a technical expert, Dr. Teller explained to the Foreign Relations Committee just what the effect of the treaty would be under such conditions. He said:

> The argument, the strongest argument, in my mind, for the treaty is to stop the spread of nuclear weapons. We have been worried about such a spread for many years, and rightfully so.
>
> We know, today, that it is easy to make nuclear explosions, and that any country that can acquire nuclear materials can make an explosion within a year. Yet is has been claimed this treaty will stop proliferation. Why?
>
> Secretary Rusk and Secretary McNamara, in their testimony, have spelled out the answer very simply and very clearly. Any nation which signs this treaty will have to test, if it tests at all, underground, and underground testing is more expensive.
>
> On this point, however, there is a simple statement I can make, a simple statement connected with dollars about which there is no doubt. An underground test of a magnitude that has been traditional for the first test of any nation, will cost approximately a million dollars. This cost, I want to make very clear, is the cost of testing. It does not include the cost of the weapon. It certainly does not include the much bigger cost of the whole development of nuclear reactors or whatever else had to be done to make the material, of the research that went into putting the material together.
>
> This million dollar figure that I mentioned to you is, I think, slightly higher, not very much higher, than the cost that would be incurred if the test were performed in the atmosphere. But no matter how these two costs compare, once a nation has gone to the expense of developing a nuclear explosive, the additional

single million dollars that is needed for underground testing will certainly not be a financial deterrent.[35]

In view of the discussion above, it would seem that the Test Ban Treaty would, at best, have very little influence on the proliferation problem. If the official government position at the time of the Senate hearings was that the treaty would retard proliferation, that optimism seemed to have disappeared a year later. In testifying in support of the Test Ban Treaty before the Senate Foreign Relations Committee, Secretary McNamara said:

> There is every reason to believe that a substantial number of nations will have the technical skills and financial resources to design, develop, and deploy nuclear weapons within the coming decade. And not only will they have the technical skills, financial resources to accomplish that, but it is very probable, in my opinion, that they would undertake such development in the absence of a Test Ban Treaty.[36]

Fourteen months after the treaty was signed, the Department of Defense released the transcript of an interview with Secretary McNamara in which he forecast that in ten to twenty years "tens of nations" would be capable of having usable nuclear weapons. He predicted that "not only will the cost of production go down dramatically, but the cost of delivery systems, such as planes and missiles, will also go down."[37] The official concern in 1964 seemed hardly less than it was in 1963. One might well wonder, then, whether the Test Ban Treaty has lessened the proliferation problem at all.

Limit the Arms Race

The fourth and final claim made for the Test Ban Treaty was that it can limit the arms race in ways advantageous to

---

[35] *Ibid.,* p. 421.
[36] *Ibid.,* p. 150.
[37] *New York Times,* October 7, 1964.

the United States. The political leadership of the nation placed particular emphasis on limiting armament because, it was argued, with modern nuclear weapons of mass destruction and their means of delivery now in the hands of nations with conflicting interests and goals, the situation has become extremely dangerous for all mankind. Further, the argument goes, increased armament results only in decreased security, and therefore the best approach to security is through disarmament. Often official spokesmen have carried this argument so far as to imply that continued development of armament would result, not in security, but in a nuclear war of annihilation. Since this appeared to be one of the prevailing arguments of the Kennedy Administration, it may have had some influence on the decision to restrict the United States 1962 test series and the urgency with which an agreement with the Soviet Union in the field of arms control was pursued after the Cuban crisis of October, 1962. The proposition that arms races lead to war seemed to be the point that President Kennedy was expressing in his address to the United Nations General Assembly on September 25, 1961, just twenty-five days after the Soviet Union breached the moratorium, and seven months before the United States began its post-moratorium test series. He said:

> For fifteen years this Organization has sought the reduction and destruction of arms. Now that goal is no longer a dream— it is a practical matter of life and death. The risks in disarmament pale in comparison to the risks in an unlimited arms race. . . .
>
> The events and decisions of the next ten months may well decide the fate of man for the next 10,000 years. There will be no avoiding those events. There will be no appeal from these decisions. And we in this hall shall be remembered either as part of the generation that turned this planet into a flaming funeral pyre or the generation that met its vow to save succeeding generations from the scourge of war. . . .

The decision is ours. Never have the nations of the world had so much to lose—or so much to gain. Together we shall save our planet—or together we shall perish in the flames.[38]

Thus President Kennedy appeared to see only two alternatives: disarmament or destruction. This same proposition was put forth by William C. Foster, Director of the Arms Control and Disarmament Agency, in an interview with the General Electric Forum on August 1, 1963, just four days before the signing of the Test Ban Treaty in Moscow. He said:

But while I think it is perfectly possible to begin turning down this race [the arms race], I cannot see just how long it will take to complete. However, the present direction is an absolute certain direction for destruction within a finite period of time.[39]

During the Senate hearings on the Test Ban Treaty, only one official witness, Dr. George B. Kistiakowsky, a member of the Advisory Board to the U.S. Arms Control and Disarmament Agency, carried the argument to this extreme, and he did so with these blunt words: "There is no end to the [arms] race, except one: war."[40] Other key Administration witnesses, Secretary of State Rusk, Secretary of Defense McNamara, Mr. William C. Foster, Dr. Harold Brown, and Dr. Herbert York, all testified to the general effect that an increase in United States nuclear power would not enhance national security, but would rather decrease it because it would be accompanied by an increase in Soviet nuclear power, and the capability for mutual destruction would become increasingly worse. They expressed hope that the Test

---

[38] "Address Before the 16th General Assembly of the United Nations," *Congressional Digest,* XLIII, 8–9 (August–September, 1964), 202, 204, 206.

[39] William C. Foster, "Interview Granted to *General Electric Forum* on August 1, 1963," *Ibid,* p. 216.

[40] *Ibid.,* p. 98.

Ban Treaty would slow the spiral without damage to relative strength, and it was generally agreed that at that time the United States was superior to the Soviet Union in strategic nuclear power.

But behind this argument, though not specifically expressed, lie two assumptions: (1) that an arms race exists, and (2) that arms races lead to war. But at the same time this argument for disarmament was advanced the Administration also confirmed its determination to maintain strategic forces superior to those of the Soviet Union. For example, Secretary McNamara told the Foreign Relations Committee: "The sum of these statements is that the United States has nuclear superiority. We are determined to maintain that superiority."[41] In other words, what the Administration seemed to feel was necessary was *both* arms control and arms superiority; and that the absence of either would create an extremely dangerous situation.

Thus the Administration was struggling with the eternal pitfall of disarmament plans: in a world of sovereign states with conflicting goals and interests, how can disarmament be reconciled with security? In the past, eras of peace have been brought about, not by disarmament, but by a preponderance of power in the hands of a peace-keeping nation. The well-known examples are the *Pax Romana*, the *Pax Britannica*, and the freedom from all-out war the world has enjoyed since the end of World War II because of the preponderance of strategic power in the hands of the United States. This has often been called the *Pax Americana*. This being the case, the efficacy of the Test Ban Treaty as a device to enhance the national security through turning down the arms race would seem, to a large degree, to depend upon the military and technological implications of the treaty, which were examined in Chapter VI above and found to be unfavorably

---

[41] *Ibid.*, p. 98.

weighed against the security interests of the United States. This would seem to be enough, in itself, to discount the claim that the Test Ban Treaty will turn down the arms race in ways advantageous to the United States; however, there is another consideration that deserves examination, and that is the relationship between strategy, on the one hand, and arms control or disarmament measures and arms races on the other. Unfortunately, the Senate hearings hardly touched upon this important subject.

The Relationship Between Arms Control, Arms Race, and Strategy

There is no question that the goals and the interests of the United States and the Soviet Union are in conflict. Because of this conflict the United States is determined to maintain strategic superiority and, indeed, strategic superiority is essential to the United States for four reasons: (1) the far-flung defensive commitments of the United States require it to be able to defend the entire Free World at one time if need be; (2) the nonprovocative defensive posture of the United States requires its strategic forces to be large enough to absorb a surprise first strike with enough strength remaining to destroy any aggressor; (3) the counterforce strategy of the United States requires it to have enough weapons to destroy the numerous and often small enemy military targets rather than simply destroying area targets, such as cities; and (4) the damage-limiting strategy of the United States requires it to target all potential enemy military installations that could cause damage to the United States and its allies.

The Soviet Union appears equally determined to acquire strategic superiority because, if this can be accomplished, the American strategy will have been defeated, and beyond the purely military advantages of superiority, such an accomplishment would prove to the world that the Communist system had bettered the Western-liberal system in a vital area of competition.[42] But in spite of the Soviets' desire for strategic superiority over the United States, they have not yet challenged the United States to an arms race of production for the simple reason that the size of their economy and their production capacity cannot equal that of the United States. In fact, if the United States and the Soviet Union were engaged in a race of production of arms, the Soviet Union could easily be defeated and exhausted, but the Soviet Union has not been so foolish as to attempt such a race. Neither has the United States attempted to force a showdown. In testimony before the Foreign Relations Committee, Secretary Rusk recognized that the United States could exhaust the Soviet Union. He said: "I think we could do it, but I don't think we would enjoy it."[43]

Rather than risk meeting the United States head-on in an arms race, the Soviets have concentrated on the research and development of nuclear technology in an effort to make an end-run around the American production capacity and develop decisively superior weapons, while using secrecy, propaganda, clever diplomacy, and well-timed détentes to avoid alarming the United States sufficiently to provoke an arms race. At the same time they have been negotiating, since the end of World War II, to deprive the United States of its nuclear advantage through disarmament proposals and a massive propaganda campaign for peace, casting the United States in the role of an "aggressor" and an "imperialist." They have not overlooked the fact that their goal of strategic superiority can be sought via two roads, arms control or disarmament, and arms development, or a combination of the

---

[42] *See* Thomas W. Wolfe, *Soviet Strategy at the Crossroads* (Cambridge: Harvard University Press, 1964), Chapter VII, "The Doctrine of Military Superiority."

[43] *Foreign Relations Committee Hearings, op. cit.,* p. 30.

two. On the contrary, they have demonstrated a thorough understanding of both techniques in the context of their own particular circumstances at a given time. A few examples will illustrate the point.

In early 1947 the Soviet Union surprised the world by rejecting the Baruch Plan and countering with demands for a total ban on atomic weapons and the destruction of all stockpiled weapons. This was followed by successive Soviet proposals from 1947 to 1949 to reduce all conventional forces by one-third concurrently with a ban on atomic weapons. The effect of these proposals would have been to deprive the United States of its nuclear power, on which it held a monopoly, while leaving the Soviet Union with vastly superior conventional forces. The fact that these proposals were unlikely to be accepted by the United States left the Soviets free in the meantime to develop their own nuclear capability, which they did with surprising rapidity and éclat. Six years later, in May, 1955, the Soviets proposed some quite different arms control measures because their circumstances had changed. By then they had broken the United States monopoly on nuclear weapons, but were faced with rapidly growing NATO power, a rearming Germany, a rapidly growing American-sponsored alliance system, and were encircled by American air bases on foreign soil. Their arms control proposal to meet this situation called for a two-stage program beginning with a freeze of all forces, to be completed by the end of 1957. Conventional forces would be reduced to levels previously suggested by an Anglo-French plan, and elimination of nuclear forces would begin only when 75 per cent of conventional reductions were completed. Other significant provisions of the proposal were the liquidation of all military bases on foreign soil and the renunciation of the use of nuclear weapons. If this proposal had been accepted, the United States deterrent would have been eliminated, Soviet conventional superiority in Europe would have been retained, German rearmament precluded, and the Western alliance system would disintegrate with the dismantling of American overseas bases.

Another example of Soviet attempts to gain strategic superiority through arms control was the September 22, 1962, draft of a *Treaty on General and Complete Disarmament under Strict International Control*. This plan called for the destruction of all submarines, all surface ships, aircraft, and artillery pieces that could be used for nuclear strikes, and all nuclear missiles except for a limited, agreed-upon number of ICBM's, anti-missile missiles, and anti-aircraft missiles to be retained by the United States and the U.S.S.R. exclusively within their own territory. This proposal would eliminate at one stroke the bulk of American strategic delivery systems. Each side would be left with a few ICBM's, but the Soviets would be left with their very large-yield weapons while the United States would be left with an equal number of much smaller weapons. This would enable the Soviet Union to give strong support to its "wars of national liberation" without fear of effective intervention. As Soviet President Anastas Mikoyan said, the Soviet proposal would strip the imperialists of the means of "resisting the revolutionary actions of the proletariat and the peasantry."[44]

The above discussion serves to show that: (1) the United States *must* retain nuclear superiority in order to implement its strategy; (2) the only way that the Soviet Union could hope to win an arms race with the United States would be through quality, rather than quantity, of strategic systems; and (3) arms control can be at least as dangerous to the American ability to deter war as an arms race. In view of this, it seems unrealistic that there should be so much expressed fear of an arms race and so little fear of being caught in a

---

[44] Election Speech in Yerevan, Armenia, reported in *Pravda*, March 15, 1962. Translated and reprinted in *Current Digest of the Soviet Press*, April 18, 1962, p. 19.

Soviet arms control trap, which would have the same effect on American strategic superiority as losing an arms race. Further, the American ability to deter war depends upon nuclear weapons because without nuclear weapons, American and allied conventional forces cannot cope with the large conventional forces and interior lines of the Sino-Soviet bloc.

Nuclear weapons, then, serve as an equalizer in an otherwise untenable situation. Neither does any great fear of nuclear weapons seem justified, so long as the United States enjoys strategic superiority. The United States certainly is not going to initiate nuclear war, and so long as it maintains a deterrent force capable of absorbing a first strike and delivering a devastating retaliatory blow it would be utter folly to strike the United States or its allies. But if for any reason, including arms control agreements, the United States should lose its strategic nuclear superiority, its deterrent capability would diminish and there would be acute danger of a war, which the Free World could hardly hope to win. The critical danger for the United States and the entire world lies not in a hypothetical arms race, which seems unlikely to come about until the Soviet Union believes that it has both technological superiority and a greater economic and production capability, but in the loss of deterrent capability. President Johnson expressed this thought well in his "Message to Congress on Defense." He said:

> But if peace is sturdier than at any time in these two decades, it is because we—and free men everywhere—have proved preparedness to be the most effectual means of preserving peace.[45]

It would seem, therefore, that to argue that arms races lead to war and that the world has a choice only of disarmament or destruction is, from the point of view of both past experience

---

[45] "The President's Message to Congress on Defense," January 18, 1965. Printed in *Washington Post,* January 19, 1965.

and the current situation, an exaggeration that could be dangerously misleading.

The treaty seems to fit the pattern of the Soviets' arms control proposals in that it enhances their efforts to make an end-run around United States production capacity by striving for technological superiority in nuclear weapons. Prior to their massive 1961–62 test series, they were not interested in stopping nuclear tests; however, when they saw their test series had resulted in significant technological advantages over the United States, they quickly agreed to the Test Ban Treaty in order to ensure retention of these advantages. The Test Ban Treaty will enable the Soviet Union to quantify its qualitative advantages at a time of its own choosing. It is interesting to note that the Soviets themselves told the world that this was the strategy behind the Test Ban Treaty in *Pravda* on August 21, 1963, while the Senate was holding hearings on the treaty. The official statement said:

> Yes, the position of the Soviet Union on the question of ending nuclear weapons tests did not become fossilized; it adapted itself to changes in the deployment of forces on the international arena, to the success in strengthening the defense potential of the USSR and that of all countries of the socialist community, and took into account everything which, in its totality, is called the realities of the nuclear age.
>
> In the first years when nuclear weapons appeared in the U.S. arsenal, when the United States had a nuclear monopoly —in view of which the security of the socialist countries was endangered—the Soviet Government proceeded from the idea that the main task was to deprive the United States of that advantage. That aim could be achieved either by completely banning nuclear weapons—which would have been tantamount to taking away these weapons from the only nuclear power of that time, the United States—or through developing our own nuclear weapons, which would help ensure the security of all socialist countries.
>
> It was at that time that the Soviet Government advanced

the demand for banning and destroying nuclear weapons, and when this demand was rejected by the Western Powers, it started to develop its own nuclear weapons, which were called upon to become a good additional guarantor of the independence and security of all countries of the socialist community, to make the imperialists lose their taste for aggression against the socialist states. Naturally, the banning of nuclear weapons without simultaneous destruction of those weapons in the possession of the United States in those years would not have been in the interests of the socialist states; it would have brought to a halt the work on developing nuclear weapons in the Soviet Union and perpetuated the U.S. nuclear monopoly.

But the situation did not remain unchanged. As a result of intensive efforts on the part of the Soviet people, of Soviet scientists, in developing their own nuclear weapons, the American nuclear monopoly was smashed, the world socialist system received its own nuclear shield, the imperialist powers lost the material basis for conducting a policy of nuclear blackmail, a policy of "from position of strength" vis a vis the socialist countries. This also put into a new perspective the question of the nuclear weapons test ban. Now the continuation of nuclear testing could lead the spiral of nuclear arms race only higher and higher, a situation in which the socialist countries as well as all peace-loving states are not interested. At the same time, with the new balance of forces, the nuclear test ban would perpetuate not the American nuclear monopoly but the fact of its liquidation, not the unilateral advantage of the imperialist camp but the new balance of strength in the sphere of nuclear weapons.[46]

The Test Ban Treaty does, of course, inhibit the qualitative aspects of weapons development and thus will have a limiting effect on arms competition. But this limitation works to the advantage of the Soviet Union in its drive to achieve technological superiority while imposing no limits on future

---

[46] "Statement of the Soviet Government, August 21, 1963," translated and reprinted in *Current Soviet Documents,* September 2, 1963, pp. 7–8.

arms production. The result is that Soviet technological advantages are preserved so that, at a time of their choice, they may well be able to transform these advantages into superior weapons. This kind of limiting of the arms race, or any future arms race, can hardly be considered an advantage to the United States, or a step in the direction of peace. Thus the fourth and final advantage claimed for the Test Ban Treaty, upon close examination, appears to be a success for a well planned and executed Soviet strategy in which the political, military, technological, and economic factors have all been carefully considered and integrated.

chapter 9

CONCLUSIONS

In light of the analysis developed in the foregoing chapters, it must be concluded that the Nuclear Test Ban Treaty was a serious mistake and a threat to the future security of the nation. In Chapter VI it has been shown that, from the military and technological point of view, there are twenty-three risks or disadvantages to the treaty with no compensating advantages. Further, the United States is more severely constrained by the treaty's restrictions on nuclear testing than is the Soviet Union. The safeguards demanded by the Joint Chiefs of Staff for the purpose of reducing the military risks of the treaty were found to be useful insofar as they commit the political leadership of the nation to a vigorous nuclear policy within the confines of the treaty, but no matter how vigorously the four safeguards are pursued they serve to ameliorate, but not eliminate, only three of the twenty-three military and technological risks. The other twenty remain unchanged.

Some proponents of the treaty, recognizing that it portends certain military and technological disadvantages, argued that its political advantages might outweigh these disadvantages. Chapter VIII examined the political advantages officially claimed for the treaty, and they were found to be unpersuasive. One, the fallout danger, can only be considered a hoax; a second, concerning nuclear proliferation, has been shown to be of little validity; the other two, when subjected to careful analysis, proved to be disadvantages rather than advantages. Politically, as well as militarily, the Nuclear Test Ban Treaty is a net liability for the United States.

In the Senate, two committees conducted hearings on the treaty and rendered reports. The Foreign Relations Committee hearings were shown to be rather superficial. The committee report concluded that: "The balance of risks in a limited test ban—the possible advantages and disadvantages to the United States and, indeed, to Western Civilization—appears to favor the treaty."[1] The Preparedness Investigating Subcommittee, however, conducted a more thorough inquiry into the military aspects of the treaty and concluded that: "From the evidence we are compelled to conclude that serious—perhaps even formidable—military and technical disadvantages to the United States will flow from the ratification of the treaty."[2] This study, then, supports the conclusions of the Preparedness Investigating Subcommittee and goes further to show that the political advantages officially claimed for the treaty turn into a net disadvantage under analysis.

From the Soviets' point of view, however, the treaty was a significant accomplishment in their struggle to overcome the American lead in nuclear technology. Starting with no nuclear capability in 1946, for seventeen years they parried and countered Western arms control proposals with one hand, while with the other they worked feverishly at the laboratories and the testing grounds until they felt that their position vis à vis the United States in nuclear technology was favorable. Then, and only then, did they agree to a nuclear test ban treaty. Significantly, the partial nuclear test ban proposal advanced by the United States on August 27, 1962, was very similar to the treaty signed on August 5, 1963, but the Soviet Union summarily rejected this proposal. Why were they ready to stop testing in the summer of 1963 but not one year earlier?

---

[1] U.S. Senate, Committee on Foreign Relations, *Executive Report No. 3, The Nuclear Test Ban Treaty,* 88th Cong., 1st Sess., 1963.

[2] U.S. Senate, Committee on Armed Services, *Interim Report by Preparedness Investigating Subcommittee on the Military Implications of the Proposed Limited Nuclear Test Ban Treaty,* 88th Cong., 1st Sess., 1963, p. 2.

The answer seems obvious. In the summer of 1962 neither the Soviet Union nor the United States had completed its second post-moratorium test series, and therefore the relative state of the art was still unclear. But in December, 1962, the Soviets completed their second post-moratorium series and by late spring or early summer they had analyzed the results and assessed their position vis à vis the United States. It was clear that for the first time the Soviet Union led the United States in certain significant aspects of nuclear technology and, according to General Le May, Dr. John Foster, and Dr. Edward Teller, they may lead in all aspects. The Test Ban Treaty will serve to preserve their newly won advantages and at the same time afford them the opportunity to overcome any leads in the lower and medium ranges that the United States might hold.

The first great break for the Soviet Union in its struggle to achieve superiority in nuclear technology came in 1958 with the moratorium on nuclear testing. During this thirty-four-month period Soviet scientists and military planners were hard at work preparing for the largest, most intense, and objectively oriented series of tests the world has ever seen. During the same period the United States virtually ceased all preparation for nuclear testing in spite of many outstanding requirements for further knowledge, and permitted its organizations, skills, and facilities to decay. Then on September 1, 1961, when the Soviet Union breached the moratorium, the United States was caught flatly unprepared. But rather than respond with maximum effort and determination, the United States mounted only a timid, half-hearted effort, conducted under such severe nontechnical restrictions that the Soviet effort was ten times the size of the corresponding American effort. The Soviet Union challenged the United States to a race for knowledge, but the United States refused to keep pace. This, of course, has had a great impact on the comparative levels of technology, which, in turn, will have an impact on the quality and effectiveness of both offensive and defensive systems of the future.

There is no question that the United States must maintain strategic nuclear superiority and the official policy is to do so. President Kennedy, President Johnson, Secretary of State Rusk, and Secretary of Defense McNamara have confirmed this policy time and time again. But this study has shown that the Nuclear Test Ban Treaty is inconsistent with the policy of strategic nuclear superiority. The United States has fallen into what Earl Voss has called *Nuclear Ambush: The Test Ban Trap*.

On the political side of the question, Professor Robert Strausz-Hupé has described the problem well. He said:

> The present policies of the United States, aiming at a peaceful accommodation with the Soviets and the relaxation of tensions through arms control and arms reduction, would be sensible policies—had certain things happened which have not yet happened. *If* we were decidedly superior to the Soviets in military hardware; *if* Soviet society had transformed itself into so many other-directed Scarsdales, Main Lines, Westchesters and Santa Monicas; *if* Premier Khrushchev trembled at China's nuclear might; *if*, and *if*, then the policies which we now pursue would probably be the right ones. Since these happy events have only occurred in our imagination, our illusory policies may well lead us into disaster.[3]

---

[3] Robert Strausz-Hupé, "Toward a World Under Peace and Freedom," in Wesley W. Posvar (ed.), *American Defense Policy* (Baltimore: Johns Hopkins Press, 1965), p. 24.

APPENDICES

APPENDICES

Test Ban Treaty Principal Witnesses

Name and Position or Organization	Foreign Relations	Armed Services	Key
Anderson, Adm. George W., Chief of Naval Operations		X	X
Andrews, Stanley M., Director, Americans for National Security	X		
Bauman, Robert E., National Chairman, Young Americans for Freedom	X		
Behre, C. Edward, Director, Cooperative League of the U.S.A.	X		
Betts, Maj. Gen. A. W., Director, Division of Military Applications, Atomic Energy Commission		X	X
Booth, Maj. Gen. Robert H., Chief, Defense Atomic Support Agency, D.O.D.		X	X
Bradbury, Dr. Norris E., Director, Los Alamos Scientific Laboratory, A.E.C.	X	X	X
Brennen, Dr. Donald G., Hudson Institute	X		
Brown, Dr. Harold, Director, Defense Research and Engineering, D.O.D.	X	X	X
Burke, Adm. Arleigh, former Chief of Naval Operations		X	X
Carey, James B., labor union executive	X		
Clinton, Col. Roy J., Deputy Chief of Staff, Weapons Effects and			

Name and Position or Organization	Foreign Relations	Armed Services	Key
Tests, Defense Atomic Support Agency		X	X
Cousins, Norman, Editor, *Saturday Review*	X		
Dean, Arthur, former Chairman of the U.S. Delegation to the Nuclear Test Ban Conference	X		
Deykin, Daniel, M.D., Physicians for Social Responsibility	X		
Dyson, Freeman J., American Federation of Scientists	X		
Foster, Dr. John S., Jr., Director, Lawrence Radiation Laboratory, A.E.C.	X	X	X
Foster, William C., Director, U.S. Arms Control and Disarmament Agency		X	X
Gottlieb, Sanford, National Committee for a Sane Nuclear Policy (SANE)	X		
Haworth, Dr. Leland J., Commissioner, A.E.C.		X	X
Hutchinson, Mrs. Aileen, Women Strike for Peace	X		
Kistiakowski, Dr. George B., Advisor to U.S. Arms Control and Disarmament Agency	X		
LeMay, Gen. Curtis E., Chief of Staff, U.S. Air Force	X	X	X
Libby, Dr. Willard F., former Chairman, A.E.C.	X		X
Long, Dr. Franklin A., U.S. Arms Control and Disarmament Agency	X		X

Name and Position or Organization	Foreign Relations	Armed Services	Key
McDonald, Adm. David J., Chief of Naval Operations	X	X	X
McIntire, Carl, International Council of Christian Churches	X		
McNamara, Hon. Robert S., Secretary of Defense	X		X
Meany, George, AFL and CIO	X		
Meselson, Matthew, Council for a Livable World, Harvard University	X		
Morris, Robert, former Chief Counsel, Senate Internal Security Subcommittee	X		
Neilen, Edwin P., Chamber of Commerce of the U.S.	X		
Pillion, Hon. John R., U.S. Congressman from New York	X		
Power, Gen. Thomas S., Commander-in-Chief, Strategic Air Command		X	X
Reissig, Herman F., Council for Christian Social Action, United Church of Christ	X		
Rice, Andrew E., American Veterans Committee	X		
Rothchild, Brig. Gen. J. H., United World Federalists	X		
Rusk, Hon. Dean, Secretary of State	X		X
Schlafly, Mrs. Phyllis, private citizen	X		
Schriever, Gen. Bernard A., Commander, Air Force Systems Command		X	X

Name and Position or Organization	Foreign Relations	Armed Services	Key
Seaborg, Dr. Glenn T., Chairman, A.E.C.	X		X
Shoup, Gen. David M., U.S. Marine Corps	X		X
Shulman, Marshall D., Professor of International Politics, Fletcher School of Law and Diplomacy	X		X
Stassen, Harold E., former Disarmament Negotiator	X		
Strauss, Adm. Lewis L., former Chairman, A.E.C.	X		
Strausz-Hupé, Robert, Director, Foreign Policy Research Institute	X		X
Taylor, Gen. Maxwell D., Chairman, Joint Chiefs of Staff	X	X	X
Teller, Dr. Edward, Consultant, U.S. Air Force	X	X	X
Twining, Gen. Nathan F., Chairman, the Twining Committee, and former Chairman of the Joint Chiefs of Staff		X	X
Warburg, James P., retired banker and scholar	X		
Watson, Arthur, Friends Committee on National Legislation	X		
Weaver, Rev. E. Paul, Church of the Brethren	X		
Wheeler, Gen. Earle G., Chief of Staff, U.S. Army	X	X	X
Wilcox, Dr. Francis O., National Council of the Churches of Christ	X		

Name and Position or Organization	Foreign Relations	Armed Services	Key
York, Dr. Herbert, former Director of Defense Research and Engineering	X		X

Foreign Relations Committee Hearings

Date	Members Present*	Other Senators Present	Sessions	Open or Closed†
August 12	29	7	2	Open
August 13	25	5	2	Open
August 14	16	2	2	Open
August 15	15	3	2	P.M. Closed
August 19	16	3	2	P.M. Closed
August 20	25	4	2	Open
August 21	25	1	2	Open
August 22	12	1	2	Open
August 23	4	–	1	Open
August 26	10	–	2	Open
August 27	9	–	2	Open

* The members of the Armed Services and Joint Atomic Energy Committees were invited to sit with the Foreign Relations Committee during the hearings. The total number of Senators on the three committees was thirty-eight.

† Open sessions cannot receive classified information.

Preparedness Investigating Subcommittee of the Armed Services Committee Hearings

Date	Members Present	Other Senators Present	Sessions	Open or Closed*
May 15	7	–	2	Closed
May 27	7	–	2	Closed
May 28	4	–	1	Closed
June 5	4	–	1	Closed
June 25	3	–	2	Closed
June 26	7	–	1	Closed
June 27	5	–	1	Closed
August 1	6	6	2	Closed
August 2	6	6	1	Closed
August 9	7	3	2	Closed
August 12	7	5	1	Closed
August 14	7	3	2	Closed
August 15	6	2	2	Closed
August 16	5	6	2	Closed
August 19	6	4	1	Closed
August 20	4	2	2	Closed
August 22	2	–	1	Closed
August 23	3	2	1	Closed
August 27	5	5	2	Closed

* Open sessions cannot receive classified information.

Treaty Banning Nuclear Weapon Tests in the Atmosphere, Outer Space, and Under Water

The Governments of the United States of America, the United Kingdom of Great Britain and Northern Ireland, and the Union of Soviet Socialist Republics, hereinafter referred to as the "Original Parties",

Proclaiming as their principal aim the speediest possible achievement of an agreement on general and complete disarmament under strict international control in accordance with the objectives of the United Nations which would put an end to the armaments race and eliminate the incentive to the production and testing of all kinds of weapons, including nuclear weapons,

Seeking to achieve the discontinuance of all test explosions of nuclear weapons for all time, determined to continue negotiations to this end, and desiring to put an end to the contamination of man's environment by radioactive substances,

Have agreed as follows:

ARTICLE I

1. Each of the Parties to this Treaty undertakes to prohibit, to prevent, and not to carry out any nuclear weapon test explosion, or any other nuclear explosion, at any place under its jurisdiction or control:

(a) in the atmosphere; beyond its limits, including outer space; or underwater, including territorial waters or high seas; or

(b) in any other environment if such explosion causes radioactive debris to be present outside the territorial limits of the State under whose jurisdiction or control such explosion is conducted. It is understood in this connection that the provisions of this subparagraph are without prejudice to the conclusion of a treaty resulting in the permanent banning of all nuclear test explosions, including all such explosions underground, the conclusion of which, as the Parties have stated in the Preamble to this Treaty, they seek to achieve.

2. Each of the Parties to this Treaty undertakes furthermore to refrain from causing, encouraging, or in any way participating in, the carrying out of any nuclear weapon test explosion, or any other nuclear explosion, anywhere which would take place in any of the environments described, or have the effect referred to, in paragraph 1 of this Article.

ARTICLE II

1. Any Party may propose amendments to this Treaty. The text of any proposed amendment shall be submitted to the Depositary Governments which shall circulate it to all Parties to this Treaty. Thereafter, if requested to do so by one-third or more of the Parties, the Depositary Governments shall convene a conference, to which they shall invite all the Parties, to consider such amendment.

2. Any amendment to this Treaty must be approved by a majority of the votes of all the Parties to this Treaty, including the votes of all of the Original Parties. The amendment shall enter into force for all Parties upon the deposit of instruments of ratification by a majority of all the Parties, including the instruments of ratification of all of the Original Parties.

ARTICLE III

1. This Treaty shall be open to all States for signature. Any State which does not sign this Treaty before its entry into force in accordance with paragraph 3 of this Article may accede to it at any time.

2. This Treaty shall be subject to ratification by signatory States. Instruments of ratification and instruments of accession shall be deposited with the Governments of the Original Parties— the United States of America, the United Kingdom of Great

Britain and Northern Ireland, and the Union of Soviet Socialist Republics—which are hereby designated the Depositary Governments.

3. This Treaty shall enter into force after its ratification by all the Original Parties and the deposit of their instruments of ratification.

4. For States whose instruments of ratification or accession are deposited subsequent to the entry into force of this Treaty, it shall enter into force on the date of the deposit of their instruments of ratification or accession.

5. The Depositary Governments shall promptly inform all signatory and acceding States of the date of each signature, the date of deposit of each instrument of ratification of and accession to this Treaty, the date of its entry into force, and the date of receipt of any requests for conferences or other notices.

6. This Treaty shall be registered by the Depositary Governments pursuant to Article 102 of the Charter of the United Nations.

ARTICLE IV

This Treaty shall be of unlimited duration.

Each Party shall in exercising its national sovereignty have the right to withdraw from the Treaty if it decides that extraordinary events, related to the subject matter of this Treaty, have jeopardized the supreme interests of its country. It shall give notice of such withdrawal to all other Parties to the Treaty three months in advance.

ARTICLE V

This Treaty, of which the English and Russian texts are equally authentic, shall be deposited in the archives of the Depositary Governments. Duly certified copies of this Treaty shall be transmitted by the Depositary Governments to the Governments of the signatory and acceding States.

IN WITNESS WHEREOF the undersigned, duly authorized, have signed this Treaty.

DONE in triplicate at the city of Moscow the fifth day of August, one thousand nine hundred and sixty-three.

For the Government of the United States of America:

DEAN RUSK

WAH

For the Government of the United Kingdom of Great Britain and Northern Ireland:

HOME

H

For the Government of the Union of Soviet Socialist Republics:

A. GROMYKO

A.G.

Existing Requirements for Nuclear Testing

Objective of Test	Effect of the Treaty
1. Determination of survivability of hardened missile launch complexes to close-in high yield explosions	preclude
2. Response of hardened underground structures to ground motion and shock wave propagation	impede
3. Verification of design criteria for hardened missile launch complexes	preclude
4. Determination of high yield effects data	preclude
5. Study of radar blackout phenomena	preclude
6. Study of communications blackout phenomena	preclude
7. Determination of warhead vulnerability to ballistic missile defense	preclude
8. Reduction of warhead vulnerability	impede
9. Determination of lethality of ABM warheads	preclude
10. Development of optimum ABM warhead	preclude
11. Development of very high yield weapons equal to or surpassing Soviet achievements	preclude
12. Further development of very low yield tactical weapons	little
13. Reduction of fission to fusion ratio	little
14. Reduction of yield to weight ratio	impede
15. Development of cleaner weapons	impede
16. Full scale operational tests of ICBM's	preclude
17. Full scale operational tests of ABM's	preclude
18. Yield verification tests of stockpiled weapons up to one megaton	little

	Objective of Test	*Effect of the Treaty*
19.	Yield verification tests of weapons over one megaton	preclude
20.	Troop training exercises using nuclear weapons	preclude

Letter from the Deputy Secretary of Defense to Senator Russell, August 23, 1963*

THE DEPUTY SECRETARY OF DEFENSE,
Washington, D.C., August 23, 1963

Hon. RICHARD B. RUSSELL,
Chairman, Committee on Armed Services,
U.S. Senate.

DEAR MR. CHAIRMAN: This letter responds to your letter of August 15 transmitting the motion adopted by the Preparedness Investigating Subcommittee on August 14 asking for information on the four safeguards that will be maintained by the administration in order to avoid injury to our national security in connection with the test ban treaty.

As the chairman of the subcommittee recognized in his colloquy with General Taylor on August 14 when the motion was under discussion, the matters referred to in the motion not only transcend the responsibilities of the JCS but also transcend the responsibility of the Department of Defense. For that reason, this reply has been prepared after obtaining advice from the Joint Chiefs of Staff and after consultation with the Atomic Energy Commission, the Central Intelligence Agency, and the Arms Control and Disarmament Agency.

When the motion was under discussion in the August 14 hearing of the Preparedness Investigating Subcommittee, it was recognized that the response, dealing with the four subjects, would have to be primarily in terms of the "criteria" or "standards" which are guiding the executive branch. I am glad to bring together here in one document the extensive assurances which have been given on the four subjects by the President, and by the Secretary of Defense and the Chairman of the Atomic Energy Com-

---

* U.S. Congress, Senate, Preparedness Investigating Subcommittee, *Military Implications of the Proposed Limited Nuclear Test Ban Treaty,* 88th Cong., 1st Sess., pp. 16–22.

mission. Furthermore, we have included here, or in a separate classified annex where appropriate, specific detail and explanation in an effort to be as fully responsive as time and circumstances permit.

Safeguard (a).—"The conduct of comprehensive, aggressive, and continuing underground nuclear test programs designed to add to our knowledge and improve our weapons in all areas of significance to our military posture for the future."

On this subject, the President, in his message of August 8, 1963, transmitting the treaty to the Senate, said: "The United States has more experience in underground testing than any other nation; and we intend to use this capacity to maintain the adequacy of our arsenal. Our atomic laboratories will maintain an active development program, including underground testing, and we will be ready to resume testing in the atmosphere if necessary. Continued research on developing the peaceful uses of atomic energy will be possible through underground testing." Later in the same message, the President referred to "our determination to maintain our own arsenal through underground tests." In his press conference last Tuesday, the President described the program of the last 2 years and added: "[W]e are going to continue to carry on, as I've said, a vigorous series of tests."

Secretary McNamara and Dr. Seaborg, in their testimony before the Senate Foreign Relations Committee on August 13 and 14, reiterated these points and elaborated on them. General Taylor, in his testimony on August 15 before the same committee, testified that the President's position on this matter had been effectively communicated.

The underground test program will expand over that currently programmed for fiscal year 1964. Details of the program are set forth in the separate, classified annex.

The Government will apply the following criteria, or standards, in the area of underground testing:

The underground test program will be comprehensive. Therefore, it will be revised to include as many as feasible of the objectives of the tests which we would otherwise do under conditions of unrestricted testing.

The underground test program will be vigorous. It will proceed at a pace that will exploit to the fullest the capabilities of existing AEC and DOD weapons laboratories. If these capabilities are proved to be inadequate to meet established requirements, they will be expanded.

The underground test program will be a continuing program designed to insure the highest practicable rate of progress in nuclear technology.

The standards established governing the type and magnitude of tests to be conducted will not be more restrictive than the spirit of the treaty limitations.

Safeguard (b).—"The maintenance of modern nuclear laboratory facilities and program in theoretical and exploratory nuclear technology which will attract, retain, and insure the continued application of our human scientific resources to these programs on which continued progress in nuclear technology depends."

There are three major facilities in which programs in theoretical and experimental nuclear warhead design technology are currently conducted and seven major DOD laboratories engaged in nuclear weapons effects research. The AEC facilities operating under contract with the Atomic Energy Commission are:

Los Alamos Scientific Laboratory, Los Alamos, N. Mex.

Lawrence Radiation Laboratory, Livermore, Calif.

Sandia Laboratory, Albuquerque, N. Mex.

The major DOD laboratories are:

Air Force Cambridge Research Laboratory, Bedford, Mass.

Air Force Weapons Laboratory, Kirtland Air Force Base, N. Mex.

Armed Forces Radiobiological Research Institute, Bethesda, Md.

Ballistics Research Laboratory, Aberdeen, Md.

Naval Ordnance Laboratory, White Oak, Md.

Naval Radiological Defense Laboratory, San Francisco, Calif.

Nuclear Defense Laboratory, Edgewood, Md.

Efforts to "attract, retain, and insure the continued application of our human scientific resources" to the programs of these laboratories depend primarily on their authorized programs and their equipment and facilities.

The AEC laboratories have been conducting programs of research in chemistry, physics, metallurgy, computer technology, and biological sciences, in addition to their major efforts in the design and development of nuclear weapons. They are also conducting development and exploration in applied nuclear physics such as reactors, controlled thermonuclear reactions, peaceful uses of nuclear explosives, nuclear propelled rockets and the development of a nuclear ramjet.

The DOD laboratories have been conducting programs of basic research in the nuclear weapons effects areas which have military applications. In addition to making effects measurements during nuclear test series, research includes studies of airblast effects on ground equipment and aerospace systems, initial nuclear radiation measurements, shielding effects, protective structures, biomedical effects, underwater effects, electromagnetic effects, and integrated effects and phenomena.

To support all of these studies extensive simulation techniques and computer facilities are used.

These activities are expected to be more than sufficient to provide the necessary stimulus and challenge to attract and retain first-rate scientific talent.

The next most important requirement after the quality of the research program necessary to maintain laboratory vitality is the physical plant with which the scientists must work. A continuous program of upgrading equipment and facilities has been underway at these laboratories since their inception, and this program is planned to continue. The approximate capital investment at each of the laboratories at the end of fiscal year 1963 was: Los Alamos, $226 million; Lawrence Radiation Laboratory, Livermore, $118 million; and Sandia, $122 million. The approximate capital investment in support of the weapons effects program of the seven major DOD weapons effects laboratories is $153 million.

Some important facilities are now under construction at the laboratories or are awaiting fiscal year 1964 appropriations. If additional facilities should be needed at these installations in order to carry out the vigorous and imaginative testing program which we have discussed, funds for such facilities will be requested.

In addition to program and facilities development, the laboratories have aggressive personnel development activities including provision for in-service training, sabbatical leave, and outside educational opportunities at affiliated universities.

The President, Secretary McNamara, and Dr. Seaborg have all expressed the firm commitment of the administration to maintaining the quality and the vitality of our weapons laboratories.

The President in his press conference last Tuesday referred specifically to the safeguard "that we should keep our laboratories activated and vital." He said, "I've already met with Dr. Foster and Dr. Bradbury; we have talked with others. We are going to do that."

Our standards in this area will be as follows:

Adequate AEC and DOD budgets, modern facilities and positive personnel policies will be maintained and augmented as necessary in order to attract and retain competent scientists in nuclear and related fields.

Broad and forward-looking research programs will be carried on which will attract and retain able and imaginative personnel capable of insuring the highest practicable rate of progress that can be attained in all avenues of potential value to our offensive and defensive posture.

Safeguard (c).—"The maintenance of the facilities and resources necessary to institute promptly nuclear tests in the atmosphere should they be deemed essential to our national security or should the treaty or any of its terms be abrogated by the Soviet Union."

The following steps are illustrative of what has been done and what is being done in this important area:

Improvement of test support facilities, including preparation and maintenance of off-continent support bases and test sites, is now underway. Approximately $55 million is now committed by AEC and DOD for fiscal year 1963 and fiscal year 1964 for improvements to Johnston Island to provide a partial oversea test capability.

To provide an airborne nuclear test capability, suitable for most weapons proof and development tests, the following needs are being satisfied: Diagnostic aircraft (being accomplished by AEC and DOD): instrumental device or weapon drop aircraft (being accomplished by AEC and DOD); sampler and other support aircraft available from the Air Force on short notice (being accomplished by DOD); suitable operating bases on Johnston Island for surveillance, weather, sampler, and sampler return aircraft (joint AEC-DOD construction underway), and in the Hawaiian area.

For a high-altitude nuclear weapons effects test capability the following steps are being taken: An oversea base at Johnston Island with adequate area and suitable facilities to support the tests, such as rocket launch pads, assembly areas, etc. (joint AEC-DOD construction underway); instrumental ships and aircraft available on short notice from the Navy and Air Force.

Further, the AEC and DOD test organization—the Nevada operations office and the Defense Atomic Support Agency, including a nucleus joint task force—will be maintained at strength. This task force will be somewhat larger than the standby unit currently maintained.

It is planned that the regular continuing laboratory programs will include development of those devices which may at some time require atmospheric testing; that the laboratories will be encouraged to carry their ideas and studies to the point where final device construction can be achieved in a time comparable to the time necessary to implement an actual atmospheric test should such tests be authorized; and that development of instruments needed for support of an atmospheric test program will be continued by the laboratories.

The President has assured the Nation that a high state of readiness to test will be maintained. In his television address on July 26, he announced, "[S]ecret preparations for a sudden withdrawal are possible, and, thus, our own vigilance and strength must be maintained, as we remain ready to withdraw and to resume all forms of testing, if we must." And in his message transmitting the treaty to the Senate he stated, "[W]e will be ready to resume testing in the atmosphere if necessary." He amplified the point in his press conference last Tuesday, stating, "Already we have begun to prepare Johnston Island for that unhappy eventuality, if it should occur. * * * [W]e are dredging the harbor, we're building some piers; there are * * * two dredges already out there, so I can assure you that we are going ahead very rapidly in that area."

The position was supported by Secretary McNamara before the Senate Foreign Relations Committee on August 13. Dr. Seaborg's remarks on August 14 were to the same effect.

On being asked how long after a treaty violation it would take the United States to begin testing, the Secretary of Defense gave the following reaction times as the objectives to be attained: Proof tests within 2 months from the decision to test, development tests within 3 months from the decision to test, and effects tests within 6 months from the decision to test. He explained that such an effects-tests readiness posture—the most difficult one to maintain—could be achieved by about a year from now.

With regard to logistics and finances, Secretary McNamara emphasized that it was important to keep up and expand the facilities on Johnston Island. He reminded that "we can provide a standby capability by utilization of the approximately $200 million in funds that the Atomic Energy Commission and the Defense Department have requested for fiscal 1964 for test purposes, and by possible supplements to those funds for further standby facilities."

The programs are designed to meet the following criteria with respect to the maintenance of a readiness-to-test posture:

The readiness-to-test program will be established on a Government-wide basis in support of a plan common to all participating agencies. The required resources and facilities will be maintained in a state of readiness, or earmarked, so that plans can be implemented within the reaction times established.

Reaction times for resumption of testing in the prohibited environments will be established and maintained within the constraints of military requirements and reasonable costs. Reaction times will vary for the broad categories of testing. As an immediate objective, we should be able to conduct proof tests of weapons in stockpile in about 2 months; operational systems tests in about 2 to 3 months; weapons development tests in about 3 months; and weapons effects tests in about 6 months.

There will be provision for periodic updating of our test program plan and for checking our readiness to test.

Safeguard (d).—"The improvement of our capability, within

feasible and practical limits, to monitor the terms of the treaty, to detect violations, and to maintain our knowledge of Sino-Soviet nuclear activity, capabilities, and achievements."

The United States now has substantial capabilities to detect, identify, and to some extent diagnose nuclear tests. These capabilities exist in the resources of our conventional intelligence community and in the resources of the atomic energy detection system (AEDS).

The role played by the intelligence community was discussed with the Senate Foreign Relations Committee on August 16 and with the Senate Preparedness Investigating Subcommittee on May 22 by Mr. McCone, Director of Central Intelligence. The intelligence community, under the direction of the U.S. Intelligence Board has increased its activities and will continue to increase its activities to cope with the new conditions under the treaty.

Secretary McNamara, in his testimony before the Senate Foreign Relations Committee on August 13, stated that: "Our examination concluded that the Soviet Union could obtain no major results by testing in the atmosphere and deep space or underwater without incurring high risk of detection and identification." He pointed out that "the only advantages of illegal testing in the three prohibited environments would be either to develop weapons with yields in the multimegaton range (since designs for weapons with yields up to 10 megatons or more can be checked by lower yield tests underground) or to determine the weapons effects of explosions which cannot be carried out at all, or not so well, underground. There will probably be no cost advantage to illegal testing in the prohibited environments because keeping the tests secret will add to the expense and difficulty of the experiments." In answer to a question about the future, Secretary McNamara referred to augmentations of the detection and identification system which have already been approved and to further augmentations which are under consideration—expanding upon the statement of the President in his message of August 8 transmitting the treaty to the Senate: "There is further assurance against clandestine testing in our ability to develop and deploy additional means of detection * * *."

Dr. Seaborg, in his summary before the same committee on

August 14, said that "systems to detect possible violation of the treaty will be maintained and continually improved."

The administration—as indicated in the detailed testimony of Defense and ACDA officials before the Senate Preparedness Investigating Subcommittee on May 9 and 15—has under consideration proposals by which our present AEDS resources can be augmented to enhance our capabilities. The proposals now being reviewed are summarized in the separate, classified annex.

The standards for the program and plans are these:

The current capability of the United States to detect and identify nuclear tests conducted by the Sino-Soviet bloc will be improved to a degree which is both feasible and remunerative. (Specific proposals for this purpose are currently under consideration.)

A vigorous research and development program will be pursued in order to improve equipments and techniques for nuclear test detection and identification.

Conventional intelligence sources will continue to complement the scientific intelligence techniques.

In conclusion, the following additional important factors must be borne in mind in connection with the concern about clandestine tests: First, the possibility of Soviet clandestine tests is lessened by the fact that they can test legally underground. Second, although there can be no guarantee that we will be able to identify all possible violations of the treaty, the Soviets cannot guarantee that we will not identify such violations. Put another way, the Soviets will never be sure of the threshold for successful evasion of our expanding and improving detection system. And, third, as the President stated in his message to the Senate of August 8, we are determined to maintain our own arsenal through underground testing and our readiness to resume atmospheric testing if the actions of others so require.

In summary, Mr. Chairman, I believe, and I trust you will agree, that the major decisions of policy have already been made and that executive action under these decisions is already going forward. I am assured—and I can assure you—that if further decisions and actions are needed, the President will take them.

Since the matters discussed above were also raised during the hearings before the Foreign Relations Committee on the test ban treaty, a copy of this letter is being furnished also to the chairman of that committee. In addition, since the contents of this letter are pertinent to an earlier inquiry from the Joint Committee on Atomic Energy, a copy is being furnished to the chairman of that committee as well.

Sincerely,

Roswell Gilpatric

BIBLIOGRAPHY

Public Documents

U.S. Arms Control and Disarmament Agency. *Disarmament: The New U.S. Initiative.* Washington: Government Printing Office, 1962.

————. *Documents on Disarmament, 1963.* Washington: Government Printing Office, 1964.

————. *Documents on Disarmament, 1962.* Washington: Government Printing Office, 1963.

————. *Documents on Disarmament, 1961.* Washington: Government Printing Office, 1962.

————. *International Negotiations on Ending Nuclear Weapons Tests: September 1961 to September 1962.* Washington: Government Printing Office, 1962.

————. *Test Ban Treaty: Questions and Answers.* Washington: Government Printing Office, 1963.

————. *Towards a World Without War: A Summary of United States Disarmament Efforts, Past and Present.* Washington: Government Printing Office, 1962.

————. *Why a Nuclear Test Ban Treaty?* Washington: Government Printing Office, 1963.

U.S. Congress, Joint Committee on Atomic Energy. *Development in Technical Capabilities for Detecting and Identifying Nuclear Weapons Tests.* 88th Cong., 1st Sess., 1963.

————. *Membership, Publications, and Other Pertinent Information of the Joint Committee on Atomic Energy.* 88th Cong., 1st Sess., 1963.

U.S. Congressional Record (daily edition), Vol. 109, 88th Cong., 1st Sess., 1963.

U.S. Department of State. *Documents on Disarmament, 1960.* Washington: Government Printing Office, 1961.

————. *Documents on Disarmament, 1945-1959.* Washington: Government Printing Office, 1960.

U.S. Senate, Committee on Armed Services, Preparedness Investigating Subcommittee. *Hearings on Arms Control and Disarmament.* 87th Cong., 2d Sess., 1962.

————. *Hearings on Military Aspects and Implications of*

Nuclear Test Ban Proposals and Related Matters. 88th Cong., 1st Sess., 1963.

————. *Interim Report on the Military Implications of the Proposed Limited Nuclear Test Ban Treaty.* 88th Cong., 1st Sess., 1963.

U.S. Senate, Committee on Foreign Relations. *Hearings on Executive M (The Nuclear Test Ban Treaty).* 88th Cong., 1st Sess., 1963.

————. *Report on Executive M (The Nuclear Test Ban Treaty).* 88th Cong., 1st Sess., 1963.

Books and Pamphlets

Beaton, Leonard, and Maddox, John. *The Spread of Nuclear Weapons.* New York: Frederick A. Praeger, 1962.

Coffey, Joseph I. *Strategy, Strategic Forces and Arms Control.* Ann Arbor: Bendix Systems Division, 1964.

Gallois, Pierre. *The Balance of Terror.* Boston: Houghton Mifflin, 1961.

Phelps, John B. *Strategy and Arms Control.* Columbus: The Mershon National Security Programs, Ohio State University, 1960.

Power, Thomas S. *Design for Survival.* New York: Coward-McCann, Inc., 1965.

Rosencrance, Richard N. *The Dispersion of Nuclear Weapons.* New York: Columbia University Press, 1964.

Articles and Periodicals

Agronsky, Martin. "Interview with Secretary Rusk and Undersecretary Harriman on the Test Ban Treaty" (July 24, 1963), *Department of State Bulletin,* August 12, 1963, pp. 240–45.

Beam, Jacob D. "A Nuclear Test Ban and Arms Control" (Speech before the Rochester Ad Club, February 28, 1963). *Department of State Bulletin,* April 1, 1963, pp. 489–93.

"Complete Text of President's Mid-Term Review on Radio-TV,"

Congressional Quarterly Weekly Report, December 21, 1962, pp. 2227–84.

Dean, Arthur H. "Statement Concerning the United States Position on Nuclear Testing to the United Nations," *Department of State Bulletin*, November 26, 1962, pp. 817–25.

Foster, William C. "The Nuclear Test Ban Issue," *Department of State Bulletin*, March 18, 1963, pp. 398–402.

Harriman, W. Averell. "Negotiating a Limited Treaty for Banning Nuclear Tests" (Speech before the National Press Club, July 31, 1963), *Department of State Bulletin*, August, 19, 1963, pp. 278–82.

Mikoyan, Anastas. "Election Speech in Yerevan, Armenia," *Current Digest of the Soviet Press*, April 18, 1962, pp. 7–8.

President's Science Advisory Committee. "Statement on the Nuclear Test Ban Treaty," *Department of State Bulletin*, September 16, 1963, pp. 430–31.

"Remarks of the President at the Signing of the Nuclear Test Ban Treaty," *Congressional Quarterly Weekly Report*, October 11, 1963, p. 1781.

Rusk, Dean. "Basic Issues Underlying the Present Crisis" (Speech delivered before the Foreign Policy Association, November 20, 1962), *Department of State Bulletin*, December 10, 1962, pp. 867–73.

———. "News Conference of May 29, 1963," *Department of State Bulletin*, June 17, 1963, pp. 931–38.

———. "News Conference of August 16, 1963," *Department of State Bulletin*, September 2, 1963, pp. 356–64.

———. "The Test Ban Treaty: Symbol of a New Course," *Department of State Bulletin*, September 2, 1963, pp. 350–56.

———. "Unfinished Business" (Address before the American Legion Convention, September 10, 1963), *Department of State Bulletin*, September 30, 1963, pp. 490–96.

———. "U.S. Efforts to Achieve Safeguarded Test Ban Treaty" (Statement before the Senate Foreign Relations Committee, March 11, 1963), *Department of State Bulletin*, April 1, 1963, pp. 485–89.

"Statement of Premier Khrushchev in Berlin, 2 July, 1963," *Current Digest of the Soviet Press*, July 31, 1963, pp. 8–9.

"Statement by the President February 12 on the Resumption of Disarmament Talks in Geneva," *Congressional Quarterly Weekly Report*, February 15, 1963, p. 213.

"Statement of the Soviet Government, August 21, 1963." Translated from *Pravda* and reprinted in *Current Soviet Documents*, September 2, 1963, pp. 3–23.

Stevenson, Adlai E. "Explanation of the United States Position on Nuclear Testing to the United Nations," *Department of State Bulletin*, October 29, 1963, pp. 635–41.

"Text of President Kennedy's January 14 State of the Union Message," *Congressional Quarterly Weekly Report,* January 18, 1963, pp. 59–62.

"Transcript of President Kennedy's Address to the United Nations," *Congressional Quarterly Weekly Report*, September 17, 1963, pp. 1692–94.

"Transcript of President Kennedy's January 24 Press Conference," *Congressional Quarterly Weekly Report*, February 1, 1963, pp. 125–28.

"Transcript of President Kennedy's February 7 Press Conference," *Congressional Quarterly Weekly Report,* February 15, 1963, pp. 210–13.

"Transcript of the President's March 6 Press Conference," *Congressional Quarterly Weekly Report*, March 8, 1963, pp. 307–9.

"Transcript of the President's March 21 Press Conference," *Congressional Quarterly Weekly Report*, March 29, 1963, pp. 455–58.

"Transcript of President Kennedy's April 24 Press Conference," *Congressional Quarterly Weekly Report*, April 26, 1963, pp. 672–76.

"Transcript of President Kennedy's May 8 Press Conference," *Congressional Quarterly Weekly Report*, May 10, 1963, pp. 727–30.

"Transcript of President Kennedy's Press Conference in Bonn," *Congressional Quarterly Weekly Report,* June 28, 1963, pp. 1073–75.

"Transcript of President Kennedy's July 17 Press Conference," *Congressional Quarterly Weekly Report,* July 19, 1963, pp. 1178–82.

"Transcript of President Kennedy's August 1 Press Conference," *Congressional Quarterly Weekly Report,* August 9, 1963, pp. 1412–15.

"Transcript of President Kennedy's August 20 Press Conference," *Congressional Quarterly Weekly Report,* August 23, 1963, pp. 1485–88.

"Transcript of President Kennedy's September 12 Press Conference," *Congressional Quarterly Weekly Report,* September 20, 1963, pp. 1661–64.

"Transcript of President Kennedy's Treaty Message to the Senate," *Congressional Quarterly Weekly Report,* August 16, 1963, pp. 1457–58.

Tyler, William R. "North America, the Open Continent," *Department of State Bulletin,* July 15, 1963, pp. 93–97.

U.S. President (Kennedy). "Letter to Senate Leaders, 11 September 1963," *Department of State Bulletin,* September 30, 1963, pp. 496–98.

U.S. President (Kennedy). "The Nuclear Test Ban Treaty: A Step Toward Peace" (An Address to the Nation on 26 July 1963). *Department of State Bulletin,* August 12, 1963, pp. 234–39.

U.S. President (Kennedy). "Nuclear Testing and Disarmament" (Radio and Television Speech Delivered March 2, 1962), *Department of State Bulletin,* March 19, 1962, pp. 445–48.

U.S. President (Kennedy). "Report on Progress of Test Ban Talks at Moscow," *Department of State Bulletin,* August 5, 1963, p. 198.

U.S. President (Kennedy). "Toward a Strategy of Peace," *Department of State Bulletin,* July 1, 1963, pp. 2–6.

SECONDARY SOURCES

Public Documents

U.S. Congress, House of Representatives. *A Compilation of Material Related to United States Defense Policies in 1962* (House Document No. 155) by Charles H. Donnelly, Legislative Reference Service, 88th Cong., 1st Sess., 1963.

U.S. Congress, House of Representatives. *United States Defense Policies in 1963* (House Document No. 335) by Charles H. Donnelly, Legislative Reference Service, 88th Cong., 2d Sess., 1964.

Books and Pamphlets

Barghoorn, Frederick C. *Soviet Foreign Propaganda*. Princeton: Princeton University Press, 1964.

Bechhoefer, Bernard C. *Postwar Negotiations for Arms Control*. Washington: Brookings Institution, 1961.

Dougherty, James E. and John F. Lehman, Jr. (eds.). *The Prospects for Arms Control*. New York: McFadden-Bartell Corp., 1965.

Hahn, Walter F. and John C. Neff. *American Strategy for the Nuclear Age*. Garden City: Doubleday Anchor, 1960.

Henkin, Louis (ed.). *Arms Control: Issues for the Public*. Englewood Cliffs, New Jersey: Prentice-Hall, 1961.

Kahn, Herman. *Thinking About the Unthinkable*. New York: Horizon Press, 1962.

Kaufman, William W. *The McNamara Strategy*. New York: Harper and Row, 1964.

Lilienthal, David E. *Change, Hope, and the Bomb*. Princeton: Princeton University Press, 1963.

McBride, James H. and John I. H. Eales. *Military Posture: Fourteen Issues Before Congress 1964*. New York: Praeger, 1965.

MacIntosh, J. M. *Strategy and Tactics of Soviet Foreign Policy*. New York: Oxford University Press, 1963.

Posvar, Wesley W. (ed.). *American Defense Policy*. Baltimore: The Johns Hopkins Press, 1965.

Voss, Earl H. *Nuclear Ambush: The Test Ban Trap*. Chicago: Henry Regnery Company, 1963.

Wolfe, Thomas W. *Soviet Influences on an Arms Control Environment*. Santa Monica, California: Rand Corporation, 1964.

———. *Soviet Strategy at the Crossroads*. Cambridge: Harvard University Press, 1964.

Articles and Periodicals

"A Ban That Could Cost Us the Arms Race," *U.S. News and World Report*, July 11, 1960, pp. 39–41.

"Administration in Center of Test Ban Crossfire," *Congressional Quarterly Weekly Report*, March 1, 1963, pp. 263–72.

Baldwin, Hanson W. "Race for the Anti-Missile Missile," *New York Times Magazine*, April 15, 1962, pp. 21–23, 96–108.

Bechhoefer, Bernard. "The Test Ban Treaty: Some Further Considerations," *Bulletin of the Atomic Scientists*, XX, 5 (May, 1964), 13–24.

"Disarmament and the Nuclear Test Ban Treaty," *On Record*, Vol. I, No. 6, 1963.

Columbia Broadcasting System. "CBS Reports: An Hour with Secretary Rusk," *Department of State Bulletin*, December 17, 1962, pp. 907–16.

"Controversy Over General and Complete Disarmament and Arms Control," *Congressional Digest*, XLIII, 8–9 (August–September, 1964), 193–224.

"C. Q. Committee Roundup," *Congressional Quarterly Weekly Report*, September 6, 1963, pp. 1533–36.

Dinnerstein, Herbert S. "Soviet Goals and Military Force," *Orbis*, V, 4 (Winter, 1962), 425–36.

"Foreign Relations Committee Approves Test Ban Treaty," *Congressional Quarterly Weekly Report*, August 30, 1963, pp. 1516–17.

"Geneva Talks Continue Amidst U.S. Political Rumbling," *Congressional Quarterly Weekly Report*, April 19, 1963, pp. 634–36.

Gerter, Michael, "New A-ICBM City Defense," *Missiles and Rockets*, January 18, 1965, p. 3.

"Is There a Defense Against the ICMB? Nike-Zeus: Suspended Sentence Before Trial," *Interavia*, XVII, 8 (August, 1962), 1016–21.

Jackson, Henry M. "Seven Assumptions That Beset Us," *New York Times Magazine*, August 4, 1963, pp. 5, 64–65.

Murphy, Charles J. V. "The Case for Resuming Nuclear Tests," *Fortune*, LXI, 4 (April, 1960), 148–50.

Murray, Thomas E. "The Case for Resuming Nuclear Tests," *World Affairs*, CXXIV, 1 (Spring, 1961), 17–20.

"Nuclear Test Ban Treaty Signed at Moscow, Transmitted to Senate for Advice and Consent to Ratification,"*Department of State Bulletin*, August 26, 1963, pp. 314–19.

"Senate Hearings Continue on Test Ban Treaty," *Congressional Quarterly Weekly Report*, August 23, 1963, pp. 1469–71.

"Should We Bomb Red China's Bomb," *National Review*, January 12, 1965, pp. 8–10.

Smith, Dale O. "How Arms Control Doctrine Can Affect U.S. Strategy," *Air Force and Space Digest*, XLV, 11 (December, 1962), 71–73, 76.

"Test Ban, Disarmament Talks Reopen Under GOP Fire," *Congressional Quarterly Weekly Report*, February 15, 1963, pp. 176, 221.

"Test Ban Hearings," *Congressional Quarterly Weekly Report*, August 16, 1963, pp. 1447–48.

"Test Ban Negotiations," *Congressional Quarterly Weekly Report,* June 14, 1963, p. 959.

"Test Ban Negotiations," *Congressional Quarterly Weekly Report,* July 19, 1963, p. 1154.

"Test Ban Treaty," *Congressional Quarterly Weekly Report*, August 2, 1963, pp. 1347–48.

Trainor, James. "DOD Says AICBM Is Feasible," *Missiles and Rockets*, December 24, 1962, pp. 14–15.

Ubell, Earl and Stuart H. Loary. "The Death of the Nike-Zeus," *Saturday Evening Post*, June 1, 1963, pp. 15–19.

"U.S. and U.S.S.R. Exchange Views on Nuclear Test Ban," *Department of State Bulletin*, February 11, 1965, pp. 198–202.

"U.S., Soviets, Britain Initial Test Ban Agreement," *Congressional Quarterly Weekly Report*, July 26, 1963, pp. 1311–12.

Wiesner, Jerome B. and Herbert F. York. "The Test Ban and Security," *Survival*, VII, 1 (January–February, 1965), 13–21.

Wolfe, Thomas W. "Khrushchev's Disarmament Strategy," *Orbis*, IV, 1 (Spring, 1960), 13–27.

INDEX